Curious England
A Guide
Volume Three

H.E. Bulstrode

Text & images copyright © 2023 H.E. Bulstrode

All Rights Reserved.

No part of this publication may be reproduced or transmitted in any form or by any means, electronic or mechanical, including photocopy, recording, or any information storage and retrieval system, without written permission from the author, except for the use of brief quotations in a review.

CONTENTS

Introduction	1
Cumbria	3
Derbyshire	37
County Durham	56
Gloucestershire	61
Northumberland	63
North Yorkshire	84
Rutland	138
Somerset	140
South Yorkshire	214
Staffordshire	222
Suffolk	235
West Yorkshire	246
Wiltshire	248
Select Bibliography	250

Introduction

As with its predecessors, this third instalment in the *Curious England* series introduces the reader to some of the lesser-known folkloric and historical curiosities of rural England, its towns, and smaller cities. If some conurbation is touched upon, it is with respect to some particular place within it, not the whole in its abstract and soulless enormity. So, here once again, I invite you to enter an enchanted realm of which we yet remain a part; one woven from lingering whispers of what once was, and plain to the eye of whosoever should care to look. And what is this stuff of which I speak? Ghost stories; tales of devilry, witchcraft, and revenants; highway robbery and murder; dragons and giants; local takes on national history; characterful carvings in wood and stone; ancient monuments and their associated folklore; and a curious tale or two that defy conventional classification.

In terms of its geographical compass, it is a somewhat motley affair, with most of the counties featured here having been touched upon in the preceding volumes, although neither Staffordshire nor South Yorkshire have hitherto made an appearance. I can only apologise for the incomplete and fragmentary nature of the coverage: such is the consequence of the piecemeal acquisition of material and its associated photography. One day, perhaps, I hope to make available fuller and more comprehensive treatments of individual counties in their own volumes, and in this respect Cumbria and Somerset are two that are set very firmly in my sights.

Please be aware that this book is neither intended to be an academic tract, nor a fully-comprehensive guide; it has been written purely for the reader's amusement, a peculiar hotchpotch hybrid spawned by memories of long ago poring over the pages of two seminal volumes that appeared in the early seventies and the late sixties: *Folklore, Myths and Legends of Britain*, published by the Reader's Digest back in 1973, and *Treasures of Britain*, published by the AA in 1968. The former is now a valuable collector's item, whereas the latter is not so highly sought after, and may be picked up for a relative song. I make no claims as to the truth or otherwise of many of the yarns related in these pages, for the nature of ghost stories and folklore more widely is such that they often defy rational explanation; those included here have been selected for their interest, and entertainment. If you happen to be familiar with a certain location, but not with the tale attached to it, be assured that I have not fabricated it, but have happened upon this peculiar nugget elsewhere; sometimes there is only a single source, whilst at other times there are many.

In writing this guide I have drawn upon so many sources that to list them all would significantly increase the length and cost of this book. I have therefore provided only a concise select bibliography, along with a selection of internet resources likely to be of particular interest to the reader. And without further ado, let me wish you well in your travels, and your exploration of this eternally curious England.

Further paperbacks published by the author include:

- *A Ghost Story Omnibus Volume Two*
- *A Ghost Story Omnibus Volume Three*
- *Uncanny Tales*
- *Anthology: Wry Out West*
- *Upon Barden Moor: An Occult Mystery*
- *Old Crotchet's Return: A Ghost Story*

Cumbria
Bew Castle, or Bewcastle Castle

If you have heard of Bewcastle, it is likely that you have done so on account of the spectacularly well-preserved Anglian cross which stands in the churchyard of St Cuthbert's. As you might guess from its name, there is a castle here too, which you might well expect to be named Bew Castle. Indeed, it appears marked as such on the Ordnance Survey map, yet some sources stubbornly name it Bewcastle Castle. The additional 'Castle' would seem to be superfluous, but then again, the parish itself is named Bewcastle, having taken its name from the fortification.

The ruined castle is but the last incarnation – the third, in fact – of a defensive structure that has stood on this site, occupying only a small corner of a once extensive Roman fort constructed to the north of Hadrian's Wall around 122 AD, and abandoned during the turbulent unrest of the fourth century. Unlike most forts of its type, it was hexagonal in shape owing to the lie of the land. Dedicated to a local deity named Cocidius, whose Roman equivalent was Mars, it was large enough to accommodate a Mithraic Temple and a bathhouse. Partial excavations here have also revealed a substantial burial ground, a number of finds from which may be viewed in Carlisle's Tullie House Museum.

Today it is hard to imagine this tranquil and isolated spot as once having been a bustling outpost of empire, occupied in the second century by the soldiers of the First Cohort of Dacians, for there is little now borne upon the wind beyond the sound of birdsong and the contented bleating of sheep. After a break of many centuries, Bewcastle resumed its importance as a border garrison in 1092, when William Rufus annexed Cumberland from Scotland. The site, with its deep wide ditch, as well as a ready source of stone from the walls of its Roman predecessor, provided all that was required for the construction of a new fortress. Its raising coincided with that of Norman castles at Carlisle and Brough, but the position of Bew Castle on the far northern margins of England led to it changing hands with Scotland a number of times. Ceded to the Scots by King Stephen whilst he battled with Mathilda for the English throne, it became part of 'the Debateable Lands', and was destroyed in 1173.

The still impressive stone walls that we see today are what remain of the third castle, built between 1361 and 1371 by John de Strivelyn, when the area was once again in English hands. During the frequent Scottish raids of the fifteenth and sixteenth centuries, it provided a welcome haven for locals seeking safety from the predations of the Border Reivers, but the area was truly a law unto itself. Thus was Thomas Musgrave reported to the Privy Council in 1602 for sheltering thieves within the castle walls, an accusation that led him to demand satisfaction from his accuser – Lancelot Carleton – with whom he subsequently fought a duel at Canonbie Holm in Dumfriesshire.

It finally ceased to be a place of defence in the 1640s, when local legend avers that Cromwell's troops subjected it to bombardment, thereby rendering it indefensible. Thereafter it suffered the fate of most abandoned castles: those materials deemed useful by the locals were taken, whilst the remainder were left to decay. And whereas its walls would seem to have withstood and deterred the assault of many a hostile force, an altogether different type of threat almost caused it to fall but a few decades ago. In 1968, a most unusual proposal was mooted: the castle would be sold off, with most of its structure journeying over the Atlantic to be raised again in America. The deal fell through, and so the castle stayed.

The Bewcastle Cross

Standing in a remote churchyard in a little-visited corner of Cumbria, the Bewcastle Cross is one of the best-preserved artefacts of the Anglo-Saxon era. It has stood where we see it today, rain-lashed and windswept, for the last 1,300 years or so, possibly a little longer, for it has variously been dated to anywhere between 675 and the first half of the following century. And yet, despite its exposure to the elements, the many centuries of weathering have failed to erase the sublime artistry of its creators. It may have lost its head, but not its heart.

To the visitor today, it may seem somewhat incongruous that a piece of art such as this should stand at such a far remove from any centre of population. Why, might you ask, would such trouble, care and expense, have been lavished on a monument where so few souls might see it? The dead in these parts are far more numerous than the living, with but a neighbouring farm and a scattering of cottages to suggest a human presence, the rough grassland here being given over to sheep; the sound of bleating being more common than that of the human voice, imparting a certain timeless quality to this near-deserted spot. But it was not always so.

Both the cross and its attendant church stand within a corner of a long-abandoned Roman fort. This outlier of imperial power, situated a few miles to the north of Hadrian's Wall, was once home to a substantial garrison, but it had long since quit its crumbled walls when the creators of the cross raised this monument to their beliefs. Who though, lived here then? And how many? Why was this spot chosen for so fine a piece?

We know the name of the man whom the cross honours, for on its west face it bears a runic inscription, one rough translation of which reads as follows:

> *This slender pillar (cross) of Hwaetred, Waethgar and Alwfwold set (it) up in memory of Alefrid, a king and son of Oswy. Pray for them, their sins and their souls.*

Was it the case, therefore, that this Alefrid may have died near here? There was, apparently, a King Alefrith who ruled over Northumbria and what is now Cumbria between 685 and 704, so it has been conjectured that it may refer to him. A further inscription on the north face of the cross refers to 'Kynibur-g' which, it has been suggested, might be a reference to a Mercian princess named Cyniburgh. These are but two of the mysteries of this unique cross, which entwine secular history with a rich biblical imagery. And although the sun shines here but infrequently, on the south face of the cross may be seen a sundial, the earliest English example to survive, albeit without its gnomon. No trace now remains of the rich colouring which once would have adorned the cross.

The Bewcastle Cross: Western Face

The Bewcastle Cross: Southern and Eastern Faces

The Bewcastle Cross: Southern Face

The Grisly Fruit of Brampton's Capon Tree

There are many Bramptons in England, but only one, so far as I am aware, which boasts a 'capon tree'. And this Brampton may be found in Cumbria. But what, might you ask, is a capon tree? It is a strange term, and there is at least one other that bears this name, although that other tree is an ancient oak that lies in Scotland not so far from Jedburgh, one of the few survivors of the almost vanished Jedforest.

So, might Brampton's Capon Tree be presumed to be one in which capons were once said to roost, or something else altogether? In France, China, and a number of other countries, you might find yourself dining upon capon – a castrated cock as overgrown as any castrato – but no longer in England. In the past, however, the flesh of the capon was a highly prized luxury. And yet, Brampton's tree once bore a more ghastly fleshly fruit, for from its branches in October 1746 swung the corpses of six men, Jacobites brought here from Carlisle Castle for the purpose of their execution. Tied to a hurdle, they were dragged through the streets of Brampton before the excited eyes of the townsfolk, eager to see that which would surely cause us to turn away – their hanging, drawing and quartering – the punishment reserved for a traitor. And so they were taken to the tree.

The Capon Tree no longer stands, but its site is marked by a stone memorial erected by subscribers in 1904. Like its Scottish namesake, the tree was an ancient oak, but when it acquired its title we do not know. It may, however, have arisen subsequent to the hanging of the six men, mockingly mutilated and deprived of their lives and manhood: ineffectual, pathetic capons. As might be expected after such a dreadful spectacle, a tradition grew up of the site of their execution being haunted, with the spirits of the Jacobites returning each year on the anniversary of their deaths. No record, however, would seem to exist of their recent return, although it was said that almost a century and a half ago, two visitors heard the rattle of the dead men's chains, and sensed their presence.

Lizzie Batey – The Brampton Witch

Local tales of witches and witchcraft often come to a bad end, but that of Brampton's witch – Lizzie Batey – proves to be something of an exception to the rule. This may in part be due to her having lived her adult life after the repeal of English laws against witchcraft in 1736, and her generally benign reputation. Indeed, her talents were such that her services were much sought after, and over time her clients came to be drawn from as far afield as fifty miles away. She was held to be a 'wise woman' in both senses of the term, and when consulted might deal with affairs as diverse as the detection of lost objects (a skill for which she was highly esteemed), the restoration of stolen property, and telling the future; young women in particular were drawn to consult her on affairs of the heart, with her never being short of business on this score. And so she made a good if not wholly respectable living over the years of her long life and, rather surprisingly for a witch, was married to a pillar of the local community: her husband John was Brampton's headmaster.

However, in other respects she played up to witchy expectations, behaving in a distinctly eccentric manner and dressing accordingly, and she most certainly was not a woman to be crossed: consequences would ensue. She is said to have warned a young woman who was about to be married that 'you'll get a white dress soon enough', and this she did, although it was not to be her wedding dress, but her funeral gown. Even winning the old woman's friendship entailed certain risks, for when she lay dying she summoned a local builder – John Parker – to her deathbed. She bequeathed him a tea set, but warned that if it were ever to leave his family, then disaster would befall whosoever acquired it. Conversely, good luck would come to all members of his family who drank from its cups. According to an article in the *Cumberland News* from December 2010, the tea set was then still in possession of the Parker family. They no longer lived in Brampton, however, but in nearby Carlisle, and its eldest member – Jim – had an interesting story of his own to tell about it.

As a young man, Jim Parker wasted no time in responding to the call to join up when war broke out in 1939, but before he set off to assume his duties with the Royal Medical Corps his mother insisted that he cycle from Carlisle to Brampton to visit a certain family member. There, he was told, he should take a drink of tea from one of the cups bequeathed to the family by Lizzie for 'good luck'. Despite his scepticism, he wished to please his mother and so did as he was told, and duly drank from the family china.

Jim's war would prove to be a long one, and he would serve until its end in 1945, and during his time in uniform he had several near misses with death. In his interview he recalled that at Salerno, the bloodiest part of the conflict in which he was involved, 'I would get these feelings as if I were being prompted to move. So I did. And then something would land on the place I had been standing – a shell.' How had he survived? His explanation was that drinking from Lizzie Batey's cup had bestowed upon him a 'sixth sense' which allowed him to dodge the shells and return home safely again. Jim Parker was a lucky man indeed, for he was one of only 37 men who returned alive out of his unit of 500.

Lizzie Batey, the Brampton Witch, passed away in early March 1817. On the day of her funeral a mighty storm blew up, and her soul was borne up and whisked away upon its howling wind. The elements themselves, some conjectured, had bent themselves to her will and responded to her call.

Brampton Marketplace

The Highwayman's Cry

The figure of the highwayman is an ambiguous one. Even during the heyday of highway robbery in the seventeenth and eighteenth centuries, there was a tendency for these gentlemen of the road to appear as romanticised rogues in popular broadsides, the tabloids of their day. And ever since they have tended to exert a somewhat salacious appeal for writers of romances and historical fiction. The reality, of course, was often rather different. How, after all, might you feel if you found yourself held up and robbed at gunpoint on your local highway today? Not too pleased, I should imagine.

The exploits of one such armed thug – John Whitfield of Cotehill in the County of Cumberland, who operated in the 1760s – lent him a certain notoriety, not only within the district, but also further afield. Such was the fear amongst the locals that they dared not venture abroad after nightfall lest they should attract his unbidden attention. He was sufficiently free with his pistol, and contemptuous of the law, as to shoot a man on horseback in broad daylight, an act which would precipitate his downfall, for a boy witnessed all and later testified against him. He was duly convicted of murder, and this is where fact and folklore would seem to diverge.

According to popular legend, Whitfield was returned to the scene of his crime – on the highway to Armathwaite – and there gibbeted alive. There, bound in his iron cage and tormented by crows, he would hang for days with neither food nor water to assuage his torment, pitiably screaming out in his agony. So insufferable did one passing coachman find his cries, that he rendered the condemned man the small mercy of discharging a shot from his pistol, his misery brought to an end upon his prompt receipt of a ball of lead. Thereafter, so the story goes, Whitfield's anguished cries for help have echoed down the centuries.

The official record, on the other hand, as reported in the *St. James's Chronicle* of 12 August 1768, presents a somewhat more prosaic picture of the condemned man's fate. Having been convicted for the murder of William Cockburn, he was duly hanged at Carlisle, and thereafter was his corpse transported to that place on the highway where his crime was committed, and there gibbeted as a sign that justice had been done, and as a warning to all who might be tempted to follow in his path. His memory was such, however, that it seems the locals would not allow it to die. Thus are his screams still said to ride the night wind. When they were last heard, and who last heard them, I do not know.

Curious Tales from Helvellyn

This is a story about one man and his dog, together with an aside about a Mosquito (the reason for the capitalisation will become clear). You may well number amongst the many tourists who have made their way to the top of England's third highest mountain, Helvellyn. If so, you can be thankful for having returned safe and sound. But not all of its visitors have been so lucky. Take, for example, Charles Gough, an artist of the Romantic period, whose fate cautions against treating the fells with anything but the utmost respect.

Whereas the peaks of the Lake District may be as pygmies to those giants of the Alps, a moment's inattention, or unsure footing, may lead to a precipitate demise. It is thus advisable, particularly for the inexperienced walker, to be equipped with suitable clothing, stout boots, a compass and a good map. After all, the broad plateau of the summit is often enveloped in a thick fog, which may descend at almost any time, making it easy to become disorientated and lose one's way. No one is more adept at navigating its perils than the trio of Fell Top Assessors whose job it is, from the onset of winter to early spring, to ascend the mountain every day to record its weather conditions, including temperature, snow depth and avalanche risk. Given his fate, we can be sure that Charles Gough would never have passed the interview.

The closing decades of the eighteenth century saw the Lake District become an increasing draw for tourists, although its blustery and rocky heights were generally shunned. All that, however, was about to change. Samuel Taylor Coleridge, for example, was a keen and pioneering fell walker who moved to Keswick in the summer of 1800. After a month in the town he found himself eager to visit his friend William Wordsworth, who had taken up residence in Grasmere. To take the road was the obvious route, but

Coleridge resolved instead to walk over the summit of Helvellyn to get there. This he did one August day, arriving at Dove Cottage at ten in the evening, prompting Wordsworth and his brother to make their first acquaintance with Helvellyn's top a matter of a few days later.

It would not be until almost five years later that Charles Gough, an artist from Manchester, would also choose to scale the mountain. Like Coleridge before him, he chose to do so alone, although it cannot be said that he was entirely without companionship, for he took with him his faithful dog, Foxie. It was on an April day in 1805 that he resolved to walk to Grasmere from the shores of Ullswater via Helvellyn, gaining the ascent via Striding Edge, a ridge that even today is well known for its difficulties. Nothing more was seen of him until a shepherd chanced to hear a dog barking some three months later in the vicinity of Red Tarn. There, at the foot of the northern slopes of Striding Edge, he found Foxie keeping guard over the body of her master, which had been reduced to little more than a skeleton. The dog had given birth to a pup, and appeared both well fed, and in good health.

It was a story and an image that exerted an instant appeal to the imagination of the Romantics, prompting the writing that year of Walter Scott's *Helvellyn* and Wordsworth's *Fidelity*. Scott's was the first to be published in 1806, with Wordsworth's effort being looked down upon at the time as the inferior of the two. Both poems celebrate the loyalty of Gough's faithful bitch, but it is Wordsworth who seeks to elevate the perceived selflessness of her devotion to a realm of almost sacred virtue to which few if any humans could hope to aspire. It would later inspire Landseer, in 1829, to paint *Attachment*, exhibited the following year alongside Walter Scott's poem in an exhibition at the Royal Academy.

And whereas extracts from both poems would come to be included in the inscription on the Gough Memorial which was raised in the memory of the dead artist in 1890, it was to be Wordsworth's verse that featured most prominently. There it still stands today, high up on Helvellyn's ridge, splotched with lichen and looking out over Red Tarn and Striding Edge, its concluding line declaring: 'In memory of that love & strength of feeling this stone was erected.' Once again, it was Gough's dog which took pride of place, but did it really deserve its reputation?

A contemporary press report from a Carlisle newspaper noted that 'The bitch had pupped in a furze near the body of her master, and, shocking to relate, had torn the cloaths from his body and eaten him to a perfect skeleton.'

Had the dog been devoted, or simply anxious to protect a convenient supply of carrion? I shall leave you to be the judge, but feel that I may have been moved to write a rather different poem of a somewhat less romantic hue.

As for Red Tarn, it seems to be misnamed for its waters are more often than not of a far darker appearance, almost black, which seems most fitting. Sitting in a bowl flanked by Striding Edge to the south, Swirral Edge and Catstye Cam to the north, and the forbidding cliffs of Helvellyn itself to the west, it looks cold and uninviting even during a day of rare warmth. Imagine then my surprise when one winter's day I saw two scuba divers emerge from its ice-rimmed shallows. They had come to investigate the remains of a Mosquito bomber that had crashed into the tarn during the Second World War. Sadly, its Australian crew had perished having collided with Striding Edge in low cloud during a night exercise on 10th February 1945. The wreckage tumbled down into the tarn, and there, for those who care to venture beneath its surface, its fuel tank may still be seen.

Red Tarn to the Left, Striding Edge to the Right

The Ghost of Hesket Hall

As with many villages in Cumbria, Hesket Newmarket was once home to a hardworking mining community. Lead and copper had been extracted from the local fells since the Middle Ages, and coal too was once mined in the parish. No longer. It is thought that the village acquired its market in the eighteenth century, but by the end of the nineteenth this had already faded into insignificance. Today, it bears little resemblance to its old self, having undergone a significant degree of gentrification, with tourism now playing the predominant role in its economy.

At some point in the second half of the seventeenth century, Hesket Hall was extensively remodelled. It is thought that there has possibly been a house on this site since the eleventh century, with certain features – such as mullioned windows – surviving from the fourteenth, but the building that presents a face to the outside world today is characteristic of the Stuart era. By the mid-1990s the house stood in a poor state of repair, and underwent extensive renovation, and although it does not seem to possess a longstanding reputation for being haunted, the Brown family, who oversaw the hall's sympathetic restoration, had something to say with respect to a certain experience of Mrs Brown's brother. It was during a visit that he found himself witness to a quite unexpected sight: that of an old woman who happened to be sharing his bedroom. She may have been wearing perfume, for when he saw her seated in a rocking chair next to the fireplace, the air bore the distinct fragrance of roses. Quite what then happened, or who she was meant to be, is not specified, but the witness was said to be a level-headed sort of chap, who would not normally entertain such fanciful notions as the existence of ghosts.

If you should find yourself in need of refreshment after a day walking the northern fells, then the village pub – The Old Crown – is highly recommended. It is Britain's first co-operatively owned pub, and possesses its own brewery. The latter, founded in 1987, boasts a delicious range of ales. There is also a challenging local walk named after the pub – 'The Old Crown Round' – which is a circular route taking in the summits of the northern fells. At 25 miles long and taking in more than 8000 feet of ascent, it starts and finishes at its door, and is thus considerably tougher than the Yorkshire Three Peaks. If you should choose to walk it, then good look.

Hesket Hall

Naworth Castle and its 'White Lady'

Naworth Castle makes for a captivating sight. It sits in a most picturesque spot to the east of the Cumbrian town of Brampton, and to the south of Lanercost Priory. Alas, it is not open to the public, except for those with exceptionally deep pockets, for one may spend the night there for the princely sum of £6,000 plus VAT. That, if anything, should long haunt your imagination, but there is also a more conventional haunting associated with this venerable pile.

Naworth possesses a lengthy history, with the stones of its initial incarnation having been laid in the thirteenth century, although there have subsequently been many changes. Thomas, the Lord Dacre who fought at Flodden, undertook extensive works during the reign of Henry VIII, and a century later, Lord William Howard would oversee a further extension of its living quarters. The last significant remodelling took place after a ruinous fire ripped through the castle in 1844, with the restoration of its interior decoration being overseen by William Morris and Edward Burne-Jones. By this time it had, of course, become a pleasant country residence, its days as the headquarters of the Lord Wardens of the Marches, dealing with the Border Reivers who bedevilled the area, then but a distant memory. In this connection it is worth mentioning that a number of Scots raiders are said to have met their ends in the castle grounds, dangling from the 'hanging tree'. It is not their nameless ghosts, however, that have come to be associated with Naworth, but the spirit of a young woman. She too is said to have suffered at the hands of one of the Lords Dacre, but her treatment could in no way be construed as having been just.

Neither names nor years are assigned to the story, just the barebones of what is claimed to have passed. The young woman was a local lass who fell in love with the then Lord Dacre. She did not, however, know of his identity, which he happily concealed for the purpose of obtaining that which he desired. And, as is the way of things, she in due course fell pregnant. It was at this point that his ardour cooled, and his identity then becoming known to her, she fell into a great despondency. Knowing that she, a girl of such lowly background and humble blood, could never aspire to marry a man of his standing, she took herself off to a stream close to the castle, and there put an end to herself. It was Lord Dacre and her mother who found the lifeless body. And the latter, in a transport of bitter grief, then cursed the man who had been the cause of her daughter's death, and those who stood to inherit in the Dacre line. He died soon after, as did his heirs in turn. Since that time, the ghost of the girl – the 'White Lady' – has been said to return to the scene of her death, unable to rest on account of having taken her own life.

Naworth Castle

The Legend of St Bega and the Founding of St Bees
It is in the very nature of the lives of the early saints that their details should be vague and their miracles suitably outlandish, and that of St Bega, after whom the village of St Bees is named, proves to be no exception. The stories that have grown up around her vary in detail, but all concur that she was an Irish princess. In a version that dates her life to the seventh century, it is said that she found herself shipwrecked hereabouts on the Cumbrian coast. Thanks to the generosity of the then Lord of Egremont, she was provided with both food and shelter, and yet it would seem

that she thought herself entitled to rather more, and thus she begged her host for a grant of land for the building of a nunnery. He was, as might be expected, somewhat taken aback by such a request, and with an air of sarcasm remarked that he would give her as much land as she found covered in snow the following day. His promise was made on Midsummer's Eve. And yet, when he awoke the next morning the land about his castle was mantled in a deep carpet of snow to the distance of three miles. Struck by such a miracle, and keen to keep his word, his promise was honoured, and he assisted her in the building of her nunnery. However, this legend is dated to no earlier than an account that was published after the Dissolution. A second, and less well-known version, can be found in a thirteenth-century manuscript entitled *Life of St Bega*.

This earlier 'snow miracle' concerned a lawsuit between the monks of the priory and a local baron named as Ranulf le Meschin (whom the historical record shows as being the brother of the actual baron, William). A dispute had arisen as to the precise extent of the priory lands, and thus a date had been set for the monks to walk their bounds and lay claim to them. On that very day it just so happened that a heavy snowfall occurred, covering all of the land in the area but that which belonged to the priory, where not a flake fell. Thus was an agreement reached as to what belonged to the priory, and what did not.

A number of other 'miracles' are also associated with St Bees. Thus in 1310 it was claimed that prayers to the saint led to the restoration of sight, speech, and sanity to those who had lost them. Others, rather more specific and told in the form of individual anecdotes, are related in the *Life of St Bega*. Amongst these feature one account concerning a Galloway thief who having mocked the saint's powers came to St Bees and stole a horse, whereupon one of the local youth's managed to aim an arrow accurately at his backside, which the visitor had dared her to shoot. Another 'miracle' concerned the horses of a group of men-at-arms which had wandered from their own pasture to graze upon the monks' crops. The monks begged them to remove their mounts, but the men sneered at the name of St Bega, only to later find their horses' hooves almost been severed from their legs. Quite why this act of violence was attributed to a dead saint rather than to the hands of aggrieved monks is rather perplexing.

As to the historical reality or otherwise of St Bega, this has been a matter of some dispute. Whereas the commonly accepted story is that she arrived at this place on the Cumbrian coast in around 650 and founded a nunnery, the earliest written sources relating to her life from some five centuries later aver that her life at St Bees was solitary. Furthermore, it has been pointed out that the Latin *Sancta Bega* translates as 'holy bracelet' casting doubt on the very existence of St Bega, for the primary holy relic associated with the saint when the Benedectine priory was founded here shortly after 1120 was a bracelet or a ring. This artefact was venerated, and on occasion, in line with pagan precedents, oaths sworn upon it, but like so many relics it disappeared during the Reformation. As with so much in the early history of Christianity in Britain, the figure of St Bega remains a tantalising mystery shrouded in myth.

The St Bees Shipwreck

Close to the seawall at St Bees is propped a rusted anchor. It marks the start of the Coast to Coast Path, which stretches all the way to Robin Hood's Bay in North Yorkshire, and was salvaged from the wreck of the SS Izaro on 25th May 2007, the centenary to the day of the ship's grounding on the Cumbrian coast. Registered in Spain, she had been carrying iron ore to Maryport, but having become lost in dense fog never reached her destination. Thankfully, no lives were lost, and the members of the Izaro's crew managed to scramble ashore where they set up makeshift home on the rocks until she was formally declared a wreck. It was then that they were able to make their way home to Bilbao. Most of the cargo was successfully salvaged, but before the last of the ore could be removed, the ship was hit by a storm and broke in two. Very little of the vessel remains today, for most of the body of the ship was cut up and sold for scrap.

St Bees Priory

The sandstone of St Bees Head is of a warm red; inviting to the eye, its surface is most pleasing to the touch when dried beneath the warming sun. It is easily carved, and over the years has thus tempted many a hand to leave its mark, with varying degrees of artistry. Here may be seen names and initials, some of lovers both living and dead, others simply declaring in their presence that a certain person was once here; a crudely cut face smiles; a cross a declaration of personal faith. What marks, if any, did the wrecked mariners of the SS Izaro leave? I find it hard to believe that none remain.

Anchor of the SS Izaro, St Bees

An Uncanny Procession and a Levy for a Fighting Cock
The town of Sedbergh, designated England's official 'book town', sits at the foot of the handsome Howgill Fells, a range familiar to any motorist who has travelled the length of the M6 between Lancaster and Penrith. Today in Cumbria, it once belonged to the West Riding of Yorkshire, and whereas nothing significant remains of its castle, its school, founded in 1525, still thrives. The town's oldest building of any note, however, is its parish church – St Andrew's. Although most of what is visible of its structure dates from around 1500, elements of the earlier building remain, it being substantially unchanged since the major renovation of 1886-7.

As for folklore, there are two rather interesting traditions associated with the town, with the church and the school possessing one apiece. Both were related by William Henderson in his book *Notes on the Folk-Lore of the Northern Counties of England and the Borders* published in 1879. With respect to St Andrew's, there once existed a belief, variants of which were, and perhaps still are, current in other parishes in the north of England, that survived here until at least the nineteenth century. This stated that if you were to visit the churchyard on All Saints Eve, then you might there bear witness to an uncanny procession led by the person of the parish clerk. Behind him would follow all the forms of those Sedbergh residents who would meet their end in the year to come. So excited by a keen and morbid curiosity was a certain Barbara Butterwith to witness this cavalcade of those condemned to die within the twelve-month, that she announced her intention to play the part of spectator to the Rev. W. Delancey Lawson. The clergyman was much alarmed at the proposal, thinking it highly inadvisable, and it was only through expending a most considerable effort that he managed to dissuade the girl from doing so, pleading the case that so ghastly a sight might set her into a panic. And how was it that Miss Butterworth came to be possessed of so fanciful a conviction? Her father was the parish clerk.

The tradition associated with Sedbergh School is altogether more earthly, with not the least smack of the supernatural about it. It was once the custom, before such a pastime was banned, for every boy to surrender to his master the sum of four and a half pence every Shrove Tuesday so that he might use the proceeds to purchase a fighting cock. As to what became of any winnings accrued from the triumph of the bird thereby purchased, no mention is made.

St Andrew's Church, Sedbergh

Stainmore: Eric Bloodaxe and a Hand of Glory

High up in the northern Pennines, on the easternmost edge of Cumbria abutting County Durham, sits the parish of Stainmore. Within its bounds lies a high Pennine pass that has long held a strategic significance, and the course of the A66 that cuts across it differs little from that of the old

Roman road. There are, perhaps, two unusual events for which Stainmore is noteworthy, one of which involved the death of a king, and another which was concerned with the foiling of a ghoulish attempt at robbery almost nine hundred years later.

Eric Bloodaxe, who had reigned as King of Norway from 931-933, later took the throne of Northumbria, which he occupied from 947-948, and then again from 952-954. His end proved to be as bloody as his name, and it was at Stainmore that he met his end. Later sources claim that he fell here in a great battle, although the consensus today is that he was more likely to have been assassinated, along with his son Haeric and his brother Ragnald. The stump of a mediaeval cross, known as the Rey Cross, may be found slightly to the east of the parish in neighbouring County Durham, and for a time it was conjectured that it might mark the spot of Eric's death or burial, but it has been moved twice from its original position and no human remains have ever been found in its vicinity. It is now simply thought to have been a boundary stone raised at the midway point between Penrith and Barnard Castle. As to Eric's final resting place, that, like the precise manner of his death, remains a mystery.

Moving forward many centuries we encounter a story of lesser significance for the course of human affairs, but one that is in many ways more peculiar, for it purports to record an instance of the use of a hand of glory. It is said to have occurred one night during the decade 1790 to 1800 at the Old Spital Inn, now a farmhouse on the A66. It was a busy hostelry at the time, and the mail coach would stop there to change horses. One evening, a traveller in the guise of a woman begged to be permitted to sleep there the night, and also requested that a bite of breakfast should be set for her so that her departure would not inconvenience the innkeeper and his family. An agreement was reached, but the innkeeper told his maid that she was to sit up until the stranger had left.

The hour being late, the girl was naturally tired. The settle by the fireside was inviting, and she lay down her head ready to sleep, but as she was about to close her eyes she once more directed them to scrutinise the caller at the inn. She felt that there was something not quite right about her, and it was then that she saw something altogether unexpected beneath the hem of the stranger's gown: a pair of man's trousers. To sleep now was quite impossible for her, but she did her best to put on a show of it: she closed her eyes and pretended to snore, watching and listening all the while. Fooled by this display, it was not long before the stranger rose up and drew something from a pocket: the severed hand of a dead man, its skin and flesh dried taut over its bony knuckles. A candle was pressed into the hand, and its fingers wrapped about it. Once the flame was flaring, the gory light was wafted about before the girl's face, a male voice intoning, 'Let those who are asleep be asleep, and let those who are awake be awake.' The magic, so thought the intruder, was complete.

Standing the hand of glory on the table, the thief turned his back on the girl and opened the outside door. Stepping outside, he descended a couple of steps and then whistled a signal to his confederates. With not a moment to lose, the maid leapt up, rushed out and pushed the thief down the steps, slamming and locking the door behind her. And yet, when she rushed to rouse the family, her screaming, shouting and shaking could not wake them, and the irate voices of the men outside grew louder and angrier. It was at this moment that it came to her what she had to do. Downstairs she hurried in search of a bowl of what was then known as 'blue' (skimmed) milk, which she threw over the hand of glory to douse its flame. Now that it was extinguished, she had no trouble in waking the members of the household, but ridding themselves of the ruffians without was not to be such an easy task. They demanded that the landlord's son return them the hand as a condition of their leaving. Their request was answered in the firm negative, reinforced with a shot from his gun. The next morning the men were gone, a lengthy trail of blood testimony to the fact that one of their number had been wounded. This unusual narrative was narrated by an old lady named Bella Parkin in 1861, whom, it was made clear, was the young girl who had thwarted the attempt to rob the Old Spital Inn.

Witchcraft, Murder, and the Haunting of Talkin Tarn

Just to the south of the market town of Brampton lies Talkin Tarn. Sitting in a glacial basin, hewn from the shattered shale by the ice, it is a picturesque spot, pleasing to the eye. Walkers, runners, anglers and birdwatchers rub shoulders with families come to enjoy ice-creams, tea, and cake, and others who hire a boat to row upon its still waters. But of those, how many, I wonder, know of the stories attached to this place? Tall tales they may be, but entertaining in their own grim way.

As with a number of lakes, this modest tarn boasts a legend of a village long lost beneath its waters, of which there is no single definitive version. However, what is common to all of the accounts that I have read is that the village was submerged on account of the uncharitable nature of its people. One version of the story has it that a stranger one day sought shelter here during a storm, but being turned away by all upon whom she called, cursed the whole lot of them with the words 'May you be flooded', and so the village and all its inhabitants were drowned. A second variant runs that Talkin was a small but prosperous place, its residents possessed of a notorious grasping avarice. And thus it was, unbeknownst to them, that they were to be subjected to a trial. A beggar arrived, and having been refused alms by all called at a house that stood away from all the rest. The old woman who lived there alone treated him kindly, and for this act of charity was spared the fate of her fellow villagers, whose wickedness was repaid by the instant coming of the waters which swallowed up drowned them all, forming the tarn that we see today.

The third version is more complex still, with the central character being Old Martha, a solitary widow, hard of hearing and living a life apart from the rest of her community. This sets it at a particular point in time too: the coming of the Black Death. This being Cumbria, the pestilence would not reach here until 1349, a year after its initial arrival in England, but it wrought its devastation here as elsewhere.

Old Martha cut a crotchety and awkward figure, and was disliked for her propensity to lavish a tongue-lashing on her neighbours. Solitary and self-sufficient, she relied upon her two cows to scrape a living, making butter and cheese which she then sold in nearby Brampton. Being of such habits and character, she garnered an ill reputation, and rumours grew that she communed with some evil force. She was shunned.

When one day she returned from Brampton, sporting a red rash that covered the whole of her neck and face, both of which were swollen, she made it clear in sharp terms that she wished for no help. And so it was that over the next few days she was seen to venture to the spring that fed the villagers' pond, her countenance hideous to behold. Shortly afterwards the villagers began to sicken. That red rash, which had left the old woman so terribly disfigured, now made its appearance upon the skin of the villagers' children: the Black Death had arrived, and it was the young that it took first. But soon the adults would suffer a like fate. Yet amongst those whom it at least for a time spared, suspicions arose as to the source of their dreadful suffering. How could it be that Old Martha, that cantankerous, venomous hag, had borne the first symptoms of this disease and yet remain alive, when it had taken the lives of their healthy and beloved children? The explanation, they believed, was obvious: she must be a witch.

She was confronted by a group of villagers who demanded that she leave them. If they drove her out, they believed, then the plague would go surely with her. Some amongst them thought this course of action not sufficient, and so the stones began to fly. She stumbled towards her home, but in doing so was struck again and fell into the water of the pond. Unable to swim, she surfaced, crying out to the villagers: 'Water! Clean water! You must use clean water!' As she had taken her water from the spring, they jumped to the conclusion that she had poisoned the pond, and thus did they pelt her with more stones until she rose no more. On the anniversary of her death, her voice is said to be heard crying out from the tarn, the waters of which had spread from the pond to engulf the dwellings of the villagers who had put her to death.

There is a further story, quite unrelated to those above, that is said to have given rise to another haunting at the tarn. In the 1850s a local lass by the name of Jessie fell in love with a local gentleman, much elevated by wealth above her station. Having used her for his pleasure, she made it clear that she would go to his mother and reveal their attachment, but he would not have it for he was engaged to another, the daughter of a rich landowner. He tried to pay her off, but she refused, and thus did he resort to a most cruel and devious plan. He lured her to the lakeside and made love to her in the shallows, and whilst in the throes of their passion, pushed her head beneath, and held it there until she drowned. His repulsive deed accomplished, he concealed her corpse in three sacks which were then deposited in a pit close to the shoreline. Her body was never found, but her terrifying and confused apparition, bathed in blood, is said to have been witnessed as it emerges from the lake.

Another ghost is said to haunt not the tarn itself, but the nearby Blacksmiths Arms, this being the spirit of a certain Maggie Stobbart who was a landlady at the pub for a time during the nineteenth century. Whereas many hauntings of this type take the form of unexplained noises, phantom footsteps, and poltergeist-like happenings, her ghostly form itself is reported as having been seen, although I am not aware of having encountered her during my visit.

Talkin Tarn

The Witch of Tebay

Tebay today is best known for its upmarket motorway services that afford fine views over the neighbouring fells, but perhaps little else. The village itself is a small place, but was smaller still before the coming of the railway, and it is for the foretelling of its coming that Mary Baynes, the Witch of Tebay, is largely remembered. After all, she died in 1811 at the age of ninety before the invention of the steam locomotive. The story goes that she told a group of local schoolchildren that horseless carriages would one day run over Loupsfell, and when the railway was eventually built, that was the route that it took. Her posthumous reputation as a prophetess was sealed, but why was she adjudged to be a witch? For less savoury reasons, it would seem.

Old Mary, as she was known, proved to be the archetypal 'repulsive' crone. She led a somewhat solitary existence, but for her cat, and had a quick temper, as well as the unusual characteristic of 'a big pocket tied upon her back.' Her neighbours regarded her with a degree of 'terror', and should their butter not set, or something ail their livestock, then she would be sure to get the blame. When the mastiff of the landlord of the Cross Keys Inn savaged Mary's cat, a man named Willan presided over its burial. He was handed a book to read from by its owner, but thinking such an observance wasted on a cat simply took the feline by its leg and said: 'Ashes to ashes, dust to dust. Here's a hole, and in thou must.' Mary reprimanded him for his levity, warning that nothing good would come of it. One day shortly afterwards when he was out ploughing his field, the plough of a sudden lurched upwards and struck him in the eye. In that instant was he blinded. How could this have happened? Why, it was plain for all in the village with eyes to see: Mary Baynes had bewitched his plough.

Derbyshire
Bakewell: The Vernon/Haddon Chapel

Bakewell's Church of All Saints is home to a remarkable collection of funeral monuments, the most striking of which commemorates Sir George and Lady Grace Manners. It stands at one end of the Vernon/Haddon Chapel, occupying the better part of the whole wall. It is a huge triple-decker structure, with its upper deck occupied by effigies of Sir George (1569-1623) and his wife Grace, née Pierrepoint (c. 1575-1650). The couple are depicted facing each other, kneeling in prayer. Whereas other memorials of its type generally depict the children of such noble couples at a much diminished scale, here they are rendered at almost the same size as their parents. On the second deck, running left to right, may be seen their stillborn son, a surviving son, and two daughters, whereas the remaining two sons and three daughters are shown on the lowermost deck. Only one of his sons – his second, John, who was to become the 8th Earl of Rutland in 1641 – survived him. When Sir George died his goods at Haddon were valued at £1,270 three shillings and fourpence.

As a young man he was not much given to learning, horsemanship being his greatest passion, but this lack of scholarship did not serve as an impediment to his entry to the House of Commons, for he was twice elected to Parliament: as an MP for Nottingham in 1588-89, and for Derbyshire, 1593-96. He acquired both seats on account of the strong political influence of the Manners family.

As for Grace, she perhaps left the people of Bakewell a more enduring legacy than her husband, for in 1636 she founded the Lady Manners School which survives to this day. She was descended, on her mother's side, from the formidable Bess of Hardwick and her husband Sir William

Cavendish. Her death mask is an eerie looking affair, and may be viewed at nearby Haddon Hall.

Monument to Sir George and Lady Grace Manners

The oldest effigy in the chapel is carved from alabaster. It represents Sir Thomas Wensley/Wendesley, who served as a Derbyshire MP on five separate occasions in the 1380s and 1390s. Fittingly, given that he was slain on 21 July 1403 whilst fighting on the Lancastrian side at the Battle of Shrewsbury, he is shown dressed in full armour. At his death he left no legitimate heir, although his illegitimate son – John Wesley – would go on to become Archdeacon of Stafford. Sir Thomas's effigy remains an impressive piece, despite its face having lost its nose, and its arms its hands.

Effigy of Sir Thomas Wensley/Wendesley (died 1403)

Sir George Vernon, who died in 1565, is commemorated by an effigy that lies sandwiched between his two wives, Margaret Tayleboys and Maud Longford. Such was his severe and harsh reputation that he was nicknamed the King of the Peak; he was not a man to cross. When his daughter Dorothy fell in love with Sir John Manners, he was dead set against the match, referring to Sir John as 'the second son of an impoverished Earl.' Love, however, was to win out: whilst her family and guests celebrated the marriage of her elder sister at Haddon Hall, she slipped out to elope with Sir John, and the couple were soon married in Leicestershire. Sir

George had no choice but to acquiesce, and so Haddon came to pass to the Manners family. The pictures below show the tombs of Sir George, and his daughter with Sir John, the latter two facing each other in prayer.

Buxton's Enchanted Beech

Trees are often held to possess magical associations, and with this in mind, the artist Andrew Frost has transformed this trunk of a dead beech into an engaging array of carvings. These depict not only animal characters from children's literature, but also representations of the Celtic god of light, Bel or Belenus, and the Romano-British goddess Arnemetia, who holds a pitcher from which flow the healing thermal waters upon which the town has founded its fortunes. The goddess's name has been interpreted as meaning 'she who dwells in the sacred grove.'

Below Belenus, with his back turned to the onlooker, is a Roman centurion, on the lookout for Brigantian raiders such as the tribesman depicted furtively peering out of the picture below. The Romans named Buxton *Aquae Arnemetiae* – the baths of the goddess of the grove – so it would seem that these springs were held sacred long before their coming.

Carvings of Belenus, Celtic God of Light, and a Centurion

The Buxton Mermaid

Not exactly the siren of myth and legend, as can be seen. No matter how many times this specimen might have cared to regard itself in the mirror and comb its scanty locks, it wouldn't have been much of a looker. This example is thought to date from the middle of the nineteenth century, and to have been made in Africa. The accompanying notes in Buxton Museum observe that 'Until recently it was thought that the Buxton mermaid was made from a monkey and a fish sewn together,' but it transpires that it is actually a rather more complex composite concoction. Examinations undertaken in 2012, which included x-rays, show that it is made from wood and wire, with teeth carved from bone, eyes of shell, its head adorned with human hair, and its tail covered in fish fins. She would appear to be a brunette.

St Alkmund of Derby

Displayed in Derby Museum and Art Gallery are two artefacts associated with St Alkmund: his stone sarcophagus, and a fragment of ninth-century cross, both of which were salvaged from St Alkmund's Church when it was finally demolished in 1968 to make way for the city's ring road.

The richly decorated stone sarcophagus, shown in the picture on the following page, once served as the receptacle for the saint's remains. He died in or around 800, aged about 30. Born a son of King Alhred/Alchred of Northumbria, the course of his life was caught up in the turbulent dynastic politics of his age, which meant that he spent more than twenty years of his brief span in exile, before returning with an army in his train. This return, however, proved to be ill-fated, for he was killed. The exact circumstances of his demise are murky, but responsibility for his death – interpreted as a 'martyrdom' – is attributed to agents acting on behalf of King Eardwulf of Northumbria. Thus did he join both his father, murdered in 774, and brother in meeting a calculated and unnatural demise.

Alkmund gained a reputation for charitable acts during his lifetime, with the poor and the orphaned being particular recipients of his largesse, and it is thought that the Mercians may have made Alkmund a saint as part of their attempt to undermine King Eardwulf of Northumbria. Following his burial in Derby, it was reported that a number of miracles took place in the vicinity of his tomb. This spot, however, was to prove to be but a temporary resting place, for early in the tenth century his remains were disinterred and moved to Shrewsbury, probably at the order of Lady Æthelflæd of Mercia, where they remained until circa 1145 when they were returned to Derby. According to legend his tomb gave out a perfume, the nature of which was not specified, as this move was taking place.

Once returned to Derby, his body rested in one of the earlier iterations of St Alkmund's Church, which was rebuilt in the 19th century, and finally demolished to make way for Derby's ring road in 1968. The demolition led to the discovery of this sarcophagus, which had lain hidden from view within the church for an unknown length of time. It had originally stood next to the altar of the 9th century church, but had been set into the floor during the 12th century leaving only the lid visible. As for the remains of St Alkmund themselves, their whereabouts is unknown.

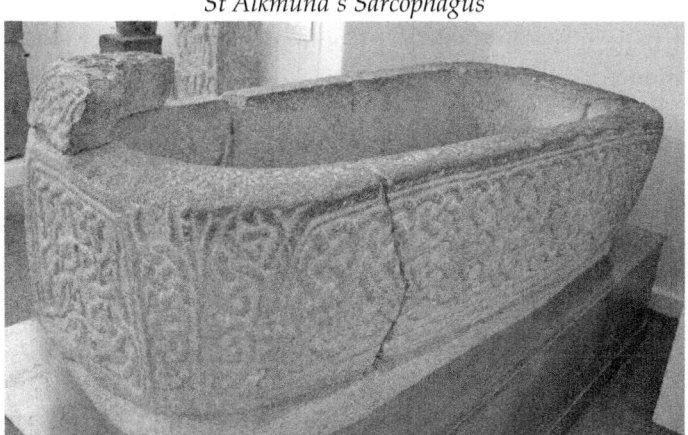

St Alkmund's Sarcophagus

Also exhibited close to the sarcophagus is the fragment of a high cross dating from around 850 which once stood outside of St Alkmund's Church. When complete it would have stood about four metres in high. It possesses four faces, each of which is richly carved.

The best preserved of the four faces, pictured on the next page but one, depicts three beasts, two of which possess incredibly long and knotted tongues, and the third sadly lacking a head. Below is a photograph of another face, in which two creatures are locked in combat beneath a classic interlacing design typical of insular artwork from this period. Another set of carvings shows what appears to be a bird above an unidentified creature, and at the very bottom what is thought to be a toad. The final face has been badly weathered, but is believed to show two or three animals knotted together. Sadly, when the cross was rediscovered in the 1840s it was then placed in the churchyard for 30 years or so, where the sulphurous effects of coalsmoke took their inevitable toll. Although presumably the cross's overall function was Christian, its iconography seems to hark back to an earlier heathen age. It must have appeared quite striking in its day, when it would also have been brightly coloured.

Detail from St Alkmund's Cross

Detail from St Alkmund's Cross

Derby Cathedral's Spiritual Host

Derby is reputedly one of the most haunted cities in Britain. The city's official website even goes so far as to claim that there have been no less than '315 sightings of ghosts in the city centre.' Small wonder then that ghost walks prove popular with certain tourists, and that it has in recent years hosted the UK Ghost Story Festival.

Derby's Cathedral was elevated from parish church to cathedral status in 1927, and proves to be something of a hub for hauntings. At least five ghosts are said to haunt the area to the rear of the building, making it rather crowded. One of these is an example of that widespread folkloric phenomenon, the white lady. Neither who she is thought to be, nor when she appears, is recorded. The second spectral manifestation claimed to frequent the area is a lachrymose lady, who carries in her arms a young child, who may, or may not, be the cause of her weeping.

The first of the male apparitions noted as calling this location 'home' is simply described as 'a man wearing old-fashioned clothing', a description open to the widest range of interpretations, so we know not whether he sports flares or a cocked hat, but the two items of apparel are highly unlikely to appear together unless the ghost should be of a somewhat confused deceased fan of Adam Ant. Perhaps the most interesting alleged haunting involves an executioner, who happened to despatch both his father and his brother (although it must be noted that the two were not one and the same man). This wretched trio share the onerous duty of unsettling whoever should cross their path, but whether they work shifts, or appear as an ensemble, is not stated.

The Georgian Interior of Derby Cathedral

Derby's Rotten Sub-Dean

This is a rare survival of a wooden effigy fashioned just before the Reformation. It is thought to date from circa 1527, and to commemorate Sub-Dean Johnson attired in the robes of a Canon of All Saints' Church, the church which would later become Derby Cathedral. When its old nave was demolished, the effigy was hidden away in the dampness of the crypt for over a century and a half, where it mouldered and rotted until it was first restored in 1880, and then again in 2010. Presumably, the Victorian restoration accounts for the carved wooden tomb chest upon which the effigy now rests. Is this a reproduction of the original? Quite possibly. The figures carved onto its side represent thirteen beadsmen, who would have been poor men of the parish paid to pray for the dead man's soul to shorten its time in purgatory, which was standard late-mediaeval practice for those who could afford it. As can be seen from the picture on the following page, the sub-dean has lost his face.

The Tomb of Bess of Hardwick

Perhaps the most impressive tomb in Derby Cathedral belongs to Bess of Hardwick. However, whereas she died in February 1608, this memorial did not come into being until 1677, having been commissioned by one of her descendants – the Duke of Newcastle.

Her life was long and eventful, with her first marriage to Robert Barlow taking place in 1543 when she was 15, and the groom was two years her junior. This first marriage lasted a little over a year, for Barlow died on Christmas Eve 1544, leaving Bess a widow until her second marriage to Sir William Cavendish in August 1547 at the age of 19. He was then Treasurer of the King's Chamber, and being 40, many years her senior. He had already been twice widowed, but she was to bear him eight children. By 1557 he too had died, but she soon married Sir William St. Loe, Captain of the Guard to Elizabeth I, for whom Bess became a Lady in Waiting. After his death in 1565, the wealth and estates that she inherited made her a wealthy and eligible widow, and she was not to marry her fourth, and last, husband – George Talbot, the 6th Earl of Shrewsbury – until 1568. Her connection to her husband's family was cemented still further by what to modern eyes would appear to be a rather unusual double wedding in February 1568, in which two of her children were married to two of his. One of her daughters – Mary Cavendish – married his eldest son Gilbert, the pair being respectively 12 and 16 years of age, whereas his daughter Lady Grace Talbot, aged only nine, became wed to Bess's son Sir Henry Cavendish who was then 18.

In 1569, the Queen entrusted the care of Mary Queen of Scots to Talbot, an onerous duty, for he had to accommodate this troublesome exile at considerable expense for the next fifteen years. Bess finally became a widow for the last time in 1590, and in the near two decades of life that remained, oversaw the construction of Hardwick Hall, and paid for the building of twelve almshouses for the poor of Derby. Her phantom is said to walk the Long Gallery at Hardwick, where it may also be glimpsed in her private apartments.

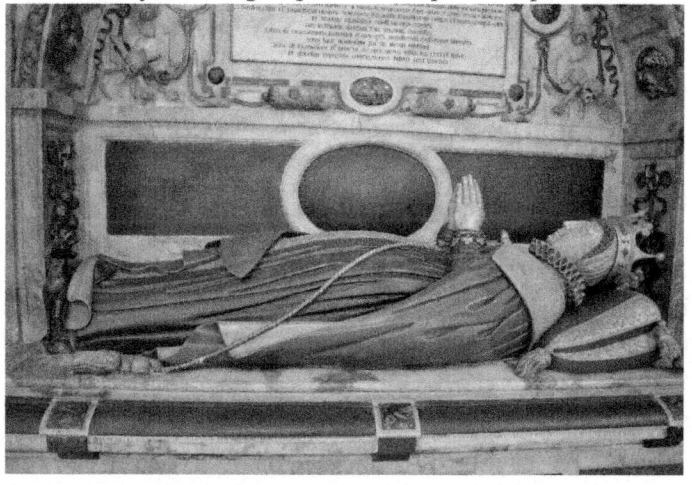

Scenic Ruins from the Industrial Past: Lumsdale

The Lumsdale Valley in Derbyshire, once a hive of industry during the boom of the first Industrial Revolution, now lies silent but for the soughing of the wind in the branches of its overarching trees, and the rush of the waters of the Bentley Brook that tumble and roar over the Lumsdale Falls. The passage of time, and the onward march of technology, have returned this place to quiet, rendering its mills picturesque prompts to the imagination. Trees thrust up amidst the ruins over which ivy creeps and spills in luxuriant growth, and fronds of light-shunning ferns bedeck the dappled woodland floor. It looks the very setting for one of L.T.C. Rolt's ghost stories, but I have no knowledge of any reputed hauntings hereabouts.

Lumsdale's heyday can be traced to the latter part of the eighteenth century, when Watts, Lowe and Co., capitalising upon the impending expiry of Richard Arkwright's patent on his water frame in 1785, built a three-storey cotton mill. To ensure an adequate and reliable source of water, the brook was dammed to form the Upper and Middle Ponds. The prosperity of the company, however, was to prove short-lived, for in 1813 it went bankrupt. The mills were then transformed into bleach works, serviced by a newly-constructed tramway. A smithy also operated at the Lower Bleach Works, with a distinctive circular trough said to have been used to quickly cool the iron rims of cartwheels, ensuring a snug fit.

However, it was not only the activities of the cotton industry to which the valley played host, for a paint mill operated here too, having its origins, it is thought, in a seventeenth-century lead mill. Corn was also ground here, and a saw mill was built in the 1850s. The valley finally fell silent in 1929, when the last of its bleach works closed down.

No longer could it be said, as commented by John Byng in 1790, that 'Every rural sound is sunk in the clamours of cotton works.' Sadly, whereas I was able to explore the valley unhindered in 2019, it would seem that access has since been closed to the public. Perhaps by the time you read this, the situation will have changed.

St Mary's Church, Tissington

St Mary's is a modest church. There is nothing grand about it. However, it cannot be said to be altogether lacking in interest. Its history is long, with the present structure dating from the twelfth century, although it underwent a heavy restoration in 1854. Both its tympanum and font survive from its founding century, with the former being flanked by two naively carved figures standing legs akimbo, their massive heads wildly out of proportion with their bodies. The beasts and figures carved into the sides of the font are of a similarly rude execution.

Moving forward some five centuries, the eye alights upon a monument to two generations of the Fitzherbert family who occupied, and indeed still do occupy, Tissington Hall, which is at but a slight remove from the church. Thankfully for the Fitzherberts, the likenesses of their forebears have been rendered with a greater degree of faithfulness and accomplishment than those of the humanoid monstrosities that grace the stonework of the Norman period. On the lower tier of the monument we see an effigy of Francis Fitzherbert (1539-1619) facing his wives Jane and Elizabeth in prayer. Above is his son John (1599-1642) facing his wife Elizabeth (died 1630). They too are shown facing each other, knelt in prayer.

Inscriptions are interposed between both sets of effigies, with a clenched fist thrusting up above the first, and an armorial shield placed over the memorial to Sir John. Although faded, the monument retains its original colour scheme, with the figures, and a number of its details, being painted. The costumes of the older generation are considerably more elaborate.

In the graveyard, if you look carefully, you will find reference to a Frank Richard Allsop on his grandfather's and father's headstone, for he was a steward who went down with the Titanic. Whereas his body remains in the depths of the Atlantic, his sister had more luck, for although she was a stewardess on the ship, she survived.

Memorial to Sir John and Elizabeth Fitzherbert

Memorial to Francis, Jane, and Elizabeth Fitzherbert

County Durham
The Cloggy of Staindrop

You can be readily forgiven for not knowing what a 'cloggy' is, and as you will see from this story, it would seem that 'Cloggy' was the name of a specific spirit said to frequent an unnamed pub in the village of Staindrop. It was first published in the June 1872 edition of the *Newcastle Magazine*, with the author voicing his gratitude to a certain Mrs Brook for having related it to him.

A number of years earlier when she was a young woman, Mrs Brook had taken a job at the said public house which entailed a variety of responsibilities, including assisting the landlady with a variety of everyday chores. One day, the latter asked her to venture upstairs to fetch down some onions, which she did. As she was coming back down the stairs, she heard quite distinctly the sound of an invisible foot treading upon each stair behind her, the sound resembling nothing less than the heavy clatter of wood upon wood; of clogs sounding upon the bare boards. Of course, she looked behind her, but there was no one to be seen. By the time that she had returned to her employer she was on the verge of fainting, which elicited nothing more than the dismissive exclamation of 'howts!' from the landlady.

Later that morning, Miss Brook, as we assume she was then called, happened to venture into another house in the village where she was asked why she looked so pale and out of sorts, whereupon she related what she had earlier experienced. The listener was forthcoming with an instant explanation: she had heard 'Old Cloggy.' Apparently, some years ago someone who had lived in the house had had a son whose mind was so disturbed that he had committed suicide by hanging. Thus was his spirit condemned to return to its former home again and again, his heavy clogs stomping the stairs. But whereas it was generally concurred that it was the sound of his footfall that most frequently manifested itself, it was not that unusual, once dusk had fallen, to catch sight of the young man's form. When Miss Brook returned to the inn and told the landlady what she had heard, her employer confessed that she knew all about the spirit, but had not mentioned it to the girl as she had not wished to alarm her. As for her own attitude towards 'Old Cloggy', well, she had heard him so frequently that he didn't bother her at all.

St Mary's Church, Staindrop

St Mary's Church has a lengthy history that can be traced back to the eighth century, and although the church has undergone extensive remodelling on numerous occasions since, the visible signs of a number of its earlier incarnations remain. But it is perhaps the monumental tombs of the Neville family that provide the most arresting sight, and a tangible link with both local and national history. One of these is unusual insofar as it is carved not from stone, but from oak. But before discussing two of these most noteworthy monuments, it is worth touching upon a peculiar speculation that arose as a consequence of works undertaken to install an early central-heating system in August 1849.

In this month a human skeleton, presumed to have been one of the Nevilles, was exhumed from beneath the floor. So far, so unexceptional you might think, but what was out of the ordinary in this case was the fact that at the feet of the skeleton the workmen had found the bones of a dog resembling those of a greyhound. Now, whereas we frequently encounter stone effigies of nobles resting their feet upon animals including dogs and lions, it is not generally thought that the deceased were buried with actual animals at their feet. In this case, it was suggested, the dog had been killed with the intent of burying it with its master. It exuded the whiff of pharaonic sacrifice. Then again, might it not have been the case that the hound proved so devoted, that when its master died it pined away, and thus was it decided to bury the loyal creature at his feet?

The two grandest tombs belonging to the Neville family are each striking in their own way, but fashioned from quite different materials. That of Ralph Neville, the 1st Earl of Westmorland (died 1425), and his two wives – Margaret Stafford and Joan Beaufort – is fashioned from alabaster, whereas the tomb of Henry Neville and his wives Anne and Jane, is wrought from oak. Both are beautifully carved, and despite not having survived the centuries unscathed, preserve much of their original artistry. It is thought that the alabaster of the earlier tomb likely came from the Staffordshire quarry of Tutbury which was owned by John of Gaunt, who was Joan's father. By the early seventeenth century respect for the tombs, and the people whom they commemorated, had declined significantly, as evidenced by the name John Smith, prefaced by the year 1620 or 1629, carved into the body of the lion upon which rest the feet of Ralph Neville's effigy.

Henry Neville died in 1564, and whereas his wives lie beside him, carvings of his children flank the tomb. The family members are, of course, interred within the vault below, but between these two fine monumental tombs is the solitary stone effigy of Margary (died c. 1343), the second wife of Ralph Lord Neville. Her feet rest upon a lion, who stares out at us, the lower part of its face, like Margary's hands, missing. Elsewhere in the church may be seen an effigy of Euphemia de Clavering, his first wife, and an effigy dating from the preceding century of Lady Isabel Neville who married Robert Fitz-Maldred in 1227. She was a Norman heiress, whereas he was the Saxon lord of Raby.

Tomb of Ralph Neville, 1st Earl of Westmorland, died 1425

Tomb of Henry Neville, died 1564

The Talking Cats of Staindrop

Seldom is it claimed that cats might speak, but in this curious little tale relating to a Staindrop farmer we encounter not one, but two talkative felines. The story goes that one night the said farmer was out walking, and when he came to cross a bridge, a cat leapt out before him and stopped him in his tracks. There it stood boldly blocking his way, and looking him straight in the eye said clear as day:

'Johnny Reed, Johnny Reed!
Tell Madame Momfoot
That Mally Dixon's deed!'

We are not told whether or not the farmer was worse the wear for drink, but the encounter certainly set him wondering. However, it was not the fact that the cat had spoken which intrigued him, but the meaning of its cryptic utterance. He pondered its meaning, but could find none. And so upon returning home he felt moved to repeat the verse aloud once more, and having done so, up shot his black cat exclaiming, 'Is she?' whereupon it promptly dashed out of the door never to return again.

The farmer, it seems, had an explanation: his puss was a fairy in feline form, and having heard of her sister's death had hurried off to her funeral, for in County Durham fairies were held to be mortal. Interestingly, William Brockie, who included this story in his 1886 publication *Legends Superstitions of the County of Durham*, notes that it bears a strong resemblance to a Danish folktale told of a 'trold' named Knurre-Murre, or Rumble Grumble.

Gloucestershire
Guiting Power's Cotswold Curiosities

As with many English villages, Guiting Power's origins stretch back into distant prehistory. Its name may be Anglo-Saxon, but it would seem to have been settled long before it acquired this particular title. A barrow dating from either the Neolithic period or the Bronze Age may be seen in a field close to the parish church. Its excavation during the 1990s caused something of a controversy owing to the removal of so great a quantity of its original structure that it had to be reconstituted using the earth that had been removed. This was done in such a neat way as to prompt at least one person to subsequently dub it a 'designer barrow'. That said, we can only be glad that Kevin McCloud of Grand Designs fame had no hand in it, for if he had we would doubtless have ended up with the barrow transformed into some monstrous open-plan box of glass and steel.

Close to the barrow in the same field may be seen the foundations of a 'Saxo-Norman' chapel, which looks to have been a very bijou structure. And then there is the parish church, in a rather better state of preservation: St Michael's and All Angels. Its two twelfth-century doorways prove that it has stood here since at least Norman times, and a small Saxon sarcophagus suggests that this site may have been in use before the Norman Conquest. Then again, it may have 'migrated' here from the nearby chapel site. Most of the building's structure, however, is later, with the tower dating from the fifteenth century, with its attractive font also dating from this time. As for its corbelled heads, I have not been able to find any dates for them, but one appears to be vomiting foliage from his mouth. The church was once in the possession of the Knights Hospitallers, whereas the surrounding lands belonged to the Knights Templar.

Until relatively recently the church stood at the centre of the village, but following the demolition of a number of buildings in the early part of the last century, it now stands on its southern edge. Other attractions in this pretty quintessentially Cotswold village include its two pubs: the Farmers Arms and the Hollow Bottom. The beer at the Farmers was good, but I didn't venture into the Hollow Bottom. I'll leave that to you.

Guiting Power Barrow

Northumberland
Alnwick Castle and its Vampire

Perhaps this title is slightly misleading, for the original tale makes no mention of either a vampire or of Alnwick. Or did it? After all, the twelfth-century chronicler William of Newburgh did set down a story concerning an individual who returned from the dead to terrorise the living, and he named its location – Anantis Castle. But where is Anantis Castle? No one knows, or at least no one knows for sure, although in 1856 Joseph Stephenson, the translator of Newburgh's *Historia Rerum Anglicarum*, suggested that Anantis most likely referred to the town of Annan in Dumfriesshire. Indeed, Annan did once have a motte and bailey castle which was built in the twelfth century, although scarcely a trace of it now remains.

It was Montague Summers in his 1929 book *The Vampire in Europe*, who not only described Newburgh's story as an early vampire account, but who also settled upon Alnwick Castle as its location. So, what follows may have taken place in Alnwick, but it could equally have been somewhere else. Whatever the case, the Alnwick Vampire has now become securely embedded in this Northumbrian town's folklore.

When William of Newburgh wrote his history in the mid-1190s, he referred to the story as having taken place in the recent past, related to him by 'an aged monk' who claims to have lived in the place where this strange course of events unfolded. The character about whom the whole of this peculiar affair revolved was described as a 'man of evil conduct' who had either fled the law, or his enemies, in York, to make a new home for himself serving at the castle (Anantis or Alnwick according to preference). Despite his change of abode, his reputation did not prosper, for that strand of evil which was ingrained in his character became ever more pronounced.

He married, but not for the better, for local gossip had it that his wife was not as faithful as she should have been. And thus did jealousy come to consume him. So tormented was he by rumours of his wife's infidelity, that he told her he was making a journey and would not be returning for many days. It was a ruse, of course, and so he came back that very evening, his maid ushering him into his wife's chamber where he hid himself on a beam where he had a good view of their marriage-bed. In time, his wife came, and lay herself down upon the bed where she did take her pleasure of a young neighbour. Enraged by that which was taking place beneath him, the husband lost his balance, and fell to the floor with a crash. The young lover was up and away that instant, whereas the jealous husband lay unconscious. When he came too, he upbraided his wife, but she pretended that what he had seen was but some sick fancy of his: she had made no sport with any lover, young or otherwise. So ill was he after his fall, that the monk who was the source of this account asked him to confess his sins, fearing that he was not long for this world. The ailing man refused, saying that he would confess the next day, but he did not live to see it. Thus did he die unshriven.

He was given a Christian burial, but his avoidance of the last rites, it would seem, did not serve him well, for he could not rest. His body crept forth from the grave at night, pursued by a hellish pack of howling hounds, as he did his rounds of both courts and houses. Fearing for their safety, the householders barred their doors, and remained within between sunset and sunrise, lest they meet the fiend. And yet their precautions did not save them, for such was the pestiferous nature of the dead man's breath and the stench of his rotting carcass, that the air of their homes was poisoned. Many died, whilst others fled. A quiet fell over the deserted town.

Those few who remained in the parish gathered on Palm Sunday, seeking consolation in the clergy. After the church service was over, two young men who had lost their father to the plague caused by this pestilential revenant stated that they would deal with the fiend once and for all. Whilst all of the other townsfolk were safely feasting in the priest's house, they would dig up the corpse, and consign it to the flames.

They hastened to the cemetery, and began frantically to dig. The corpse they found at no great depth below the earth which they could see had lately been disturbed. What they found was repulsive: they 'laid bare the corpse, swollen to an enormous corpulence, with its countenance beyond measure turgid and suffused with blood; while the napkin in which it had been wrapped appeared nearly torn to pieces.' One of the men slashed at it with his spade, and out of it 'incontinently flowed such a stream of blood, that it might have been taken for a leech filled with the blood of many persons.' Steeling themselves, they dragged the body beyond the village and hastily threw up a funeral pyre, but there was one thing that they had to do before it was lit: tear the heart from the bloated corpse. It was their belief that unless the heart was removed and destroyed, the body would burn. The spade was here employed once more to slash into the body, whereupon the heart was torn out and ripped to shreds. Now, at last made safe, the corpse was placed upon the pile of wood, and the guests rushed forth from the priest's house to watch as it was reduced to ashes. Thus were the unnatural post-mortem ramblings of the nameless man brought to a halt, and the town – perhaps Alnwick – delivered from its pestilence.

The Main Gate of Alnwick Castle

The Curse of the Dirty Bottles Inn, Alnwick

The Dirty Bottles Inn in the town of Alnwick boasts not a resident ghost, but a curse, although it is not the pub itself that is said to be cursed, but a small number of 'dirty bottles' from which it takes its name.

The hostelry, which stands close to the mighty Alnwick Castle, has operated as such since at least the early eighteenth century, although the building dates back to the 1600s or earlier, with an inverted stone shield, situated high above its main doorway bearing the de Vesci arms, thought to date from the 1200s. It was originally named the Old Cross Inn, until one day the landlord had the misfortune to touch the bottles still displayed in one of the pub's windows. No sooner had he done so than he promptly dropped down dead, whereupon his wife declared that should anyone ever again seek to lay a hand upon the bottles, or attempt to move them, then they would share her husband's fate. Thus have they stayed undisturbed, sandwiched between an inner and outer window – an early example of double glazing – since that fateful day. As to when this happened, there appears to be some confusion, for the pub's website declares it to have occurred in the nineteenth century, whereas a plaque on the inn's wall baldly states that 'These here bottles have remained untouched since 1725'.

An alternative version of the tale states that a local wise woman had once been allowed to sell her potions and tinctures which were displayed in the pub window. One day, a disagreement with the landlord led to the revocation of this right, and thus did she curse the bottles, stating that anyone who touched them would meet a sudden death. With a sardonic laugh the landlord grabbed the first bottle, and promptly dropped dead.

The Witch of Edlingham Castle

The ruins of Edlingham Castle, set in a tranquil valley amidst damp and verdant pastures, are very much off the beaten track, and unless you are either a local or come in search of them, you are unlikely ever to find them. A modest place it may be, lacking the grandeur of fellow Northumbrian fortresses such as Alnwick, Bamburgh, and Warkworth, but it is not without character. Possessed of more human and homely dimensions than its better-known contemporaries, a segment of its solar tower has come adrift, leaning at a rather alarming angle, bound to the main body of the structure by a makeshift array of connecting steel rods. Pisa, however, it is not. There are no crowds, for one, and the climate is altogether less clement.

Before its builders saw fit to raise a castle, it is thought that a manor house once stood here, but as the threat of Scottish incursions waxed over the course of the fourteenth century, it morphed into the muscular presence whose wreck we see today. Only the relatively intact solar –

completed in the middle years of the century of the Great Pestilence – presents to the onlooker a semblance of what it would once have been. Locals hungry for stone stripped it of much of its masonry in the latter part of the seventeenth century, subsequent to the peace attendant upon England and Scotland being united under the single crown of the Stuarts, if not under a single parliament.

Whatever events of note may have taken place at Edlingham over the years, the last, and least orthodox, must surely have been a witch trial that was held here in 1683. The unfortunate accused was a certain Margaret Stothard, an old woman of the parish. As to her accusers, they were two brothers – John and Jacob Mills – whom, it would seem, were prompted to instigate proceedings against Margaret by their guilty consciences.

The Mills brothers were amongst the last, if not the last, to reside at the castle, and it was whilst lying there in his bed one night that John took affright. There was a great blast of wind without his chamber, whereupon 'Something fell with a great weight upon his heart and gave a cry like a cat'. That it actually was a cat would seem the most rational explanation, but he averred otherwise, stating that at that very moment something of an otherworldly nature manifested itself at the end of his bed: a light, at the centre of which stood 'Margaret Stothard or her vision'. This would not be the only time that he would witness this vision, a sight that reduced him to such an abject state of terror that his hairs were caused to stand on end.

As for Jacob, he evidently possessed no greater regard for Margaret Stothard than his vision-prone brother, for he too sought to damn her with his testimony. He stated how she, having been refused alms by a local couple, had brandished a 'white thing' at them no less than three times. His insinuation would seem to have been that it was a wand, for the following day the daughter of this uncharitable couple fell sick, protesting that Margaret 'was pressing her like to break her back and press out her heart'. Death hastened to take her, and the girl breathed no more. Was this not proof enough of witchcraft? Seemingly eager to see the old woman hang, Jacob also informed the local magistrate, Henry Ogle, that the accused had once been called upon to cure a child. This she had duly done, demonstrating her skill by removing the illness to a calf.

What prompted the brothers' pronounced animus towards Margaret Stothard? Unlucky as she may have been to have found herself accused of witchcraft, she was fortunate insofar as witch beliefs amongst the educated were by the latter part of the seventeenth century on the wane, and Henry Ogle was not a man given readily to superstition. He threw out the case, and so she remained at liberty. It would have been interesting to learn what the magistrate thought of her accusers.

Edlingham's Church of St John the Baptist

If you should find yourself visiting Edlingham's parish church it will probably be on account of you having come to view the castle. If this should be the case, then do take a few minutes to step inside and take a look around. Given its peaceful ambience today, and the seeming absence of habitations with the exception of a neighbouring farm or two, it is difficult to imagine that Edlingham was once a thriving village of some 600 souls when it was gifted by King Coelwulf to St Cuthbert in the 8th century. Nothing of the then church survives, however, for the structure that remains today is believed to be the fourth such building which has stood on the site, with the initial two having been made of wood rather than of stone.

Even so, the church is old; very old. Fragments of the third iteration of St John's – built in stone a few years prior to the Norman Conquest – may be seen in the nave's west wall, but nothing more. There is, however, a small piece of a sculpted cross, possibly from the eighth century, resting inside the church. Whereas today's building is solidly built of stone, dating predominantly from the eleventh and twelfth centuries, its tower is slightly younger, and was probably raised in the early fourteenth. The latter is readily defensible, its narrow windows proving ideal for the use of the bow when fending off raiding parties of Scots.

Its internal arches are typical examples of the Romanesque, and set into the threshold of the inner door inside the porch may be seen carvings from two mediaeval grave slabs. There are a number of memorials to be seen on the church walls, and the east window is of stained glass, dedicated to the memory of Lewis de Crespigny Buckle who died in 1864. He was the son of the incumbent vicar, who served at Edlingham for 52 years. His death occurred far away at sea on the SS Nemesis, which had been launched in 1839 as a warship commissioned by the East India Company. The ship was significant insofar as she was Britain's first ocean-going warship built of iron. She saw action in the First Opium War (1839-42), with the Chinese dubbing her the 'Devil Ship'. Thereafter she was deployed to combat piracy in the vicinity of Indonesia and the Philippines, but returned to Belfast in 1854. How did this young Northumbrian come to meet his end? Through illness, accident, or combat? The legend on the commemorative window does not say, simply declaring 'The Sea Gave up the Dead which were in it'.

Featherstone Castle and its Wild Hunt

That Northumberland should be home to more than seventy castles is testimony to its turbulent history, which over the centuries was punctuated by numerous raids and incursions by the Scots. Whereas these events are a matter of historical record, it would seem that the popular imagination, dissatisfied with the barebones of bloodthirsty facts alone, has often invested these fortresses with additional tales of a more romantic nature, which frequently spill over into the shadowy realm of the supernatural.

Featherstone Castle enjoys a most pleasing aspect. Situated in the upper reaches of the South Tyne Valley, its extensive grounds remain unspoilt by development, and from the path along the neighbouring riverbank the walker may pause to look upon it with an appreciative eye. But in the middle of the last century the scene was not quite so appealing, marred as it was by the appearance of a purpose-built camp that served as a temporary home to some 7,000 German POWs. Precious little remains of that sad and transitory structure, whereas Featherstone Castle itself still stands.

Featherstone's origins stretch back to the twelfth century when it was a relatively modest manor house, but by 1330 it had assumed a recognisably defensive form with the addition of its pele tower. It would not be until the seventeenth century, however, that the castle would undergo a significant enlargement and modification, leaving it much as we see it today. So much for its history and the firm dates relating to its construction, but what of the origins of the stories associated with its alleged ghostly residents? These are, somewhat unsurprisingly, rather murkier.

As with so many castles and stately homes, Featherstone is said to be home to a nameless lady, with this particular example presenting herself to the onlooker in a fine gown of green and brown. She glides about its corridors, but her form has not been witnessed, or so I have read, since some point in the past century. Another ghost is said to be that of a Sir Reginald FitzUrse. Presumably, this is not the individual of that name who was one of the four knights who slew Thomas à Becket, but someone else. Whoever he was, his spirit is said to haunt one of its towers in which he had been held captive and subsequently starved to death. The third, and most complex, story connected to the castle concerns a phantom wedding party. This not-so-merry throng is said to be witnessed variously in the castle's courtyard, or riding furiously from nearby Pynkinscleugh Wood. In this latter variation we find yet another variation upon the motif of the Wild Hunt, and a most romantic and bloody one it is too.

Featherstone's phantom hunt is said to reconvene upon the anniversary (commonly held to be 17 January) of the alleged events that will here be narrated. At midnight on this date, its riders hurtle pell-mell from Pynkinscleugh Wood to the castle, its passing rumoured to drive the local dogs into a fearful frenzy. The story runs as follows.

It so happened that the only daughter of the last Baron Featherstonehaugh fell in love, and as is generally the case in such stories, it was not with the man whom her father had intended. Ridley of Hard Riding was young Abigail's desire, yet she submitted to her father's will, and thus gave her hand in marriage to another. Her husband was a distant relative, selected so as to secure an advantageous alliance in the defence of the border. On the day of her wedding, Lady Abigail and her husband went hunting with his retainers, and having crossed the bridge into Pynkinscleugh Wood in search of deer, were surprised instead to find Ridley. There he sat upon his horse at the head of his band of men, and looking down from the hillside called upon the groom to give up his bride. The latter refused, and a bloody fight ensued. In an effort to separate husband and lover, now engaged in a fight to the death, the young bride interposed herself between the two, only to fall at the point of their swords. In fury the men continued to fight over the dead Abigail, until each mortally wounded the other, and the two of them died where they had fought. Ravens flocked where

Ridley had fallen, feasting upon his blood that had pooled in a rock, which was thereafter given the name of Ravens' Rock.

The phantom hunt would make its first appearance that very eve, for when Baron Featherstone rose at midnight to greet the returning wedding party, the figures that filed silently into the hall made for a ghastly sight. This was no cause for rejoicing, indeed, for as the nobleman looked upon each he recognised them, and yet did not, for their skin was of a deathly pallor, and their bodies mutilated and torn with gaping and bloody wounds. Here he made the sign of the cross, and in that instant did the dreadful party fade from sight. Ever since, so the story goes, the phantom hunt repeats this journey from Pynkinscleugh to the castle.

In fact, there was a Lady Abigail, and a Ridley of Hard Riding too, but the lives of the two were separated by more than a century, and she married at least twice and lived into middle age. The origins of this murderous and tangled tale probably lie in events that took place on 24 October 1530, for on that day Nicolas Featherstonehaugh was murdered by two members of the Ridley family: William and Hugh.

Featherstone Castle

Thirlwall Castle: its History, Treasure, and Haunting

It wasn't the prospect of buried treasure that lured me to Thirlwall Castle, appealing as that might have been. No. It was, however, a tale connected to the said treasure, as well as a general interest in picturesque ruins, that did. Situated just to the north of the village of Greenhead, close to the route of Hadrian's Wall, Thirlwall cannot in any way be described as 'grand'. From a distance, its ruins look far from spectacular; they are, it must be said, unprepossessing in the extreme. And yet, as the visitor draws closer – much closer – it becomes apparent that rather more than the single ruined wall suggested by the view from afar has survived. It is only, however, once the eminence upon which it sits has been scaled that it fully reveals itself. Modest in size it may be, but it remains unmistakeably a castle, or, more accurately, a fortified tower, albeit it a tumbledown and inhospitable one.

For several centuries it provided a secure habitation to the Thirlwall family. Constructed largely using masonry robbed out from Hadrian's Wall, from which it stands a mere 200m, it was raised around 1330, with the earliest written reference to it dating from 1369, when it was described as a *castrum*. Perhaps the most famous family member to have hailed from this seat on the northernmost fringe of England, was Sir Percival Thirlwall, standard-bearer of Richard III at Bosworth Field. The day went badly for Sir Percival, for his legs were cut from under him, and, like his master, he did not survive to see another. It is not, however, the shade of this unfortunate lord who is said to frequent the walls of the castle, but the form of some 'hideous dwarf'.

A nineteenth-century account states that a nameless baron of the Thirlwall line once returned from the wars overseas laden with a great treasure, the most singular item of which was a table wrought from solid gold. Now, whereas we might expect such a treasure to be entrusted to a stout and sturdy guard of impressive stature, its safekeeping fell instead to the said dwarf, who executed his duty with a great zeal and diligence. At some point, a party of Scots made an appearance, and beholding the castle resolved to take it. Their numbers were such that they overwhelmed its defence, and in their storming and ransacking of Thirlwall they slew both the baron and his retainers. But this was not the prize that they had come for; they lusted after its fabled treasure, after the golden table and the bags of money they knew to be held there. And yet, no matter how hard and long they searched, they could not find it. As to why this was so, the story suggests the following. The dwarf, intent to the last on safeguarding his master's treasure, made off with it, and hurled the table and the money into a deep well. He in turn followed, and by dint of some sly act of sorcery, closed up its opening, denying the raiders of their desired plunder. It has remained lost ever since, the spirit of the dwarf keeping watch over its resting place so that none may take it. However, in the year 1793 or thereabouts, a local man found what he thought to be a well during the course of his ploughing. Knowing of the legend, he was most excited by his discovery, and thus resolved to return to that same spot under cover of darkness. But when he did so, he could find no trace of it; the well had vanished.

The only son of a widow, so some accounts run, may yet succeed in breaking the spell that binds the ghost of the dwarf to his perpetual guardianship, and thereby be rewarded with the discovery of the treasure.

History does indeed confirm that Thirlwall Castle was once occupied by the Scots, but during the Civil War in aid of the Parliamentarian cause. There is no mention of a dwarf, living or otherwise, in this connection. In either 1738 or 1748 the Thirlwall's parted with their traditional seat, selling it off to the Earl of Carlisle. Ruin was its subsequent fate. Today it may be approached by a footpath leading from a small car park on the Greenhead road. There is no entry charge. If you should be the solitary son of a lonely widow, then I wish you good luck in your quest for riches.

Warkworth: its Church, Castle, and Bridge

The village of Warkworth is a delight for anyone who savours history and English vernacular architecture, boasting many buildings built from the local yellow sandstone that exudes a warmth even on the coldest of days. In its layout, it in several respects resembles Appleby-in-Westmorland in neighbouring Cumbria, with its church situated at the bottom of the hill next to the river, with a broad historic high street sweeping up to the castle which sits at the top of the hill. And like Appleby, it has over the centuries suffered from the attentions of the Scots. They, however, were not the first to raid and pillage, for it is believed that in 875 the Danes led by Halfdan Ragnarsson destroyed the timber church that had stood here since at least the reign of King Ceolwulf of Northumbria (729-737). It was to Ceolwulf that Bede dedicated his *Historia ecclesiastica gentis Anglorum* (*An Ecclesiastical History of the English People*), the first history of the English which all others would subsequently draw upon. Sadly, owing to its preoccupation with the Church, it leaves much that we would like to know with respect to secular history unsaid. In this respect, it truly is acceptable to refer to the fifth to the eighth centuries as 'the Dark Ages', for much of our political, social, and economic life from this period remains unrecorded and unknown, lurking in the shadows cast by the 'light' of the Church.

The Church of St Laurence is first mentioned by name in 737, and would be rebuilt in stone during the ninth and tenth centuries. However, the building that occupies the site today has its origins in the early twelfth century. Despite its stout walls, designed as much for defence as for any other reason, the villagers who sought refuge there on 13 July 1174 would not be spared by the Earl of Fife, Donnchad II. Whilst King William I of Scotland was defeated and captured that day a few miles further north at the Battle of Alnwick, Donnchad led a column of Scots to Warkworth. His men proceeded to torch the village, together with the church in which some 300 souls were burned to death.

The tower was added to the church a few years later in around 1200, the spire appearing in the fourteenth century, with the structure of St Laurence's being completed pretty much as we see it today by the close of the fifteenth. Inside is an enigmatic and finely-carved effigy of an armoured knight. Dating from the fourteenth century, it rests upon a table tomb from the 1600s which bears the legend 'Sir Hugh of Morwicke who gave the Common to this Towne of

Warkworth'. The knight is not believed to be Sir Hugh. The coat of arms indicates that he was a member of the de Abulyn family which was based in Durham, but beyond that, his identity is unknown.

Unknown Knight: St Laurence's Church, Warkworth

Warkworth Castle failed to resist the Scots in 1173. It was, after all, at that time held to be 'feeble', and so it proved. By 1200, however, it had begun to assume the layout that we see today, for it, like the church, was to undergo a major programme of rebuilding. Its origins, like those of many fortresses, is obscure, but it is thought that a castle has stood here since at least the twelfth century, although there is some dispute as to who built the initial structure: the Scots, under Prince Henry of Scotland, or the English under Henry II. It has been speculated that this in turn was built on the site of a pre-existing Anglo-Saxon residence belonging to the Earls of Northumbria before the Norman Conquest. The castle makes its first documentary appearance in a charter, dated to the years 1157-1164, whereby Henry II granted Warkworth to Roger fitz Eustace. It is thought that most of the current features of the castle date from the years 1199 to 1214, and when it was besieged by the Scots in 1323, it fared far better than a century and a half earlier.

Warkworth Castle

The castle was granted to Henry Percy, the 2nd Lord Percy, in 1332. Although Alnwick was the Percys' seat of power, the family preferred to reside at Warkworth, until the seventeenth century. It was besieged by Henry IV in 1405, with his use of cannon securing a speedy surrender. The Crown then confiscated the Percys' holdings, but restored them in 1416. During the Wars of the Roses the Percys sided with the Lancastrians, Warkworth being occupied by the Yorkists under the Earl of Warwick, who from here directed the sieges of Alnwick, Bamburgh, and Dunstanburgh. With the arrest and imprisonment of the 9th Earl in 1605 for his links to the Gunpowder Plot, the castle passed to Sir Ralph Gray, under whose lease the fabric of the fortress declined. During the Civil War, it was the Parliamentarians who used it as a garrison, but when they abandoned it in 1648 they ensured that it would be useless to any rival.

Warkworth Castle

With such a turbulent and bloody history, it might be expected that the public imagination would populate the castle with a ghost or two, and so it has here in the form of one of England's many indistinct grey ladies. The grey lady in question is reputed to be the spirit of Margaret Percy (née Neville), who died at Warkworth in 1372 at the age of 33. Details of her haunting are sketchy, with little more being remarked other than that she has been witnessed wandering one of its towers, and has been heard as well as seen.

Crossing the River Coquet is what is believed to be the sole surviving example of a fortified bridge in England. Dating from the late fourteenth century, it retains its defensive gateway. Closed to traffic in 1965, its cobbles still welcome the pedestrian, with the bridge affording fine views of the river upstream, as well as the lowermost part of the village clustered about the parish church.

Fortified Gatehouse: Warkworth Old Bridge

North Yorkshire
Bedale, St Gregory's Church

Bedale is a compact and historic town in the former North Riding of Yorkshire, its parish church richly endowed with a number of items of artistic interest, despite the efforts of the Puritans to trash such symbols of papist idolatry. Thus you will find here five noteworthy stone effigies, although the identities of the two knights shown blow dressed in fifteenth-century armour are unknown owing to the destruction and defacement of their original tombs.

Effigies of Two Unknown Knights, St Gregory's, Bedale

However, we do know who the effigies of the lord and lady situated to your left as you emerge from the tower into the body of the church represent: Baron Fitzalan Knt. (died 1 June 1306) and his first wife, Muriel, who died in 1290 or earlier. He was a prominent and powerful figure who served as a Guardian of Scotland from 1291, being the brother-in-law to King John of Scotland (1292-1296) who served as an English vassal. He campaigned on behalf of Edward I in Wales in 1277 and 1287, and on the side of the king at the Battle of Falkirk in 1298, as well as at the siege of Caerlaverock Castle in 1300. He outlived all of his sons, with his estate passing to his daughters by his second marriage to Maud who died in 1297.

In the church's north chapel is a fourteenth-century effigy of a priest, and set into the floor of the north aisle is a damaged, but still striking, black marble grave slab depicting Thomas Jackson who died in 1529. However, it is also worth looking up when visiting St Gregory's, for it possesses a fine fifteenth-century wall painting of St George.

Sadly, owing to the threat of theft, a tantalising fragment of the distant past is now held locked away in the crypt, and may only be viewed by prior arrangement with the rector: Wayland's Stone. This piece of a Viking hogback gravestone was discovered in 2003, and depicts the Norse god Weland/Wayland the Smith, as well as the tail of his winged cloak that he used to escape captivity after having been lamed, his feet entangled in decorative knotwork.

Brimham Rocks: Druidic Fancies and a Lovers' Leap
Although natural and owing nothing to the human hand, the striking formations of Brimham Rocks overlooking Nidderdale in North Yorkshire (formerly the West Riding) have over the years come to attract a number of stories and associations, with some being rather more fanciful than others. During the second half of the eighteenth century, when all things druidical were very much in vogue, Brimham came to be associated with the vanished priestly caste of pre-Roman Britannia. Enthusiasts for the 'old religion' thus dubbed many of its rocks in honour of these sickle-wielding mystics, some bearing vaguely 'sensible' names such as the Druid's Altar and Druid's Idol, whereas others received anachronistic titles such as the Druid's Writing Desk, and even the Druid's Telescope. There were many more such appellations, with the advocates of Brimham as an ancient sacred site averring that although natural, some of the stones had later been modified to serve specific purposes. One, for example, possessed a hollow which, it was speculated, served as an oracle, with a druid standing unseen on one side delivering oracular pronouncements to the listener on the other.

Today, most of the rocks have come to be named after their suggestive shapes, and thus we encounter such formations as the Dancing Bear and the Baboon's Head. There is also Lovers' Leap, said to have been named after a pair of lovers who had eloped owing to the girl's father having disapproved of the match. Unfortunately for the young couple, the father is said to have pursued them to Brimham, where, unable to escape him, they joined hands and leapt from the rock named after them. Thankfully for the would-be suicides, they came to no serious harm, and the relieved and penitent father gave his consent for his daughter to marry her sweetheart. And so Julia married Edwin, although quite when this dramatic incident is said to have taken place is not recorded. There have been many further falls from the rocks over the years, but rather more through accident than design. You may also recognise them doubling up for Dartmoor from the 1988 Granada adaptation of *The Hound of the Baskervilles*, in which Jeremy Brett delivers his peerless interpretation of Sherlock Holmes.

Brimham Rocks

One of the Beast-Like Brimham Rocks

The Clapham Witch

If the picture here does not tally with the Clapham that you likely have in mind, it will be for the good reason that this particular Clapham lies not within Greater London, but in the Yorkshire Dales. And rather unusually the church that you see – the Church of St James – possesses an association with witchcraft. Quite when the story came to attach itself to the building is a matter for speculation, as the tale of the witch – Alice Ketyll – would appear to be borrowed from that of an earlier mediaeval near-namesake – variously Dame Alice Kettle or Anne Kytler – who was tried for witchcraft in Kilkenny in the 1320s. Putting this aside for the time being, the story runs as follows.

At the time of the Wars of the Roses, Dame Alice, or Auntie Ketyll, lived in a hovel in nearby Trow Ghyll. One version of the story characterises her as the foster mother of John de Clapham, who having spent all of his money on the Lancastrian cause, turned to her for assistance. Having little herself, she sacrificed nine cockerels and sold her soul to the Devil, an expedient which succeeded in conjuring up five hundred men whom he marched to York in 1468.

Alice was later tried and convicted for witchcraft, her punishment being to pay for the re-roofing of the church with lead. As her pocket could not stretch to it, she begged the local clergy to accompany her to the summit of Ingleborough. There they discovered lead and silver, and as a mark of gratitude for this unanticipated bounty they granted her a pardon, later burying her in the churchyard. Try as you might, you will not find her grave.

Little remains of the original church beyond its tower. What wasn't destroyed by invading Scots in the early fourteenth century, was extensively reworked early in the nineteenth. However, it is worth stepping inside if only to see its finely-carved pulpit.

Church of St James, Clapham

Tom Lee: Grassington's Most Notorious Son

An eighteenth-century blacksmith would have been called upon to fashion many things, amongst which must have numbered the iron cage of a gibbet when occasion called. However, given that it was Tom Lee who was Grassington's resident smith, we may well ask who was it that came to fashion his? Was it his apprentice? As to how his corpse came to be so displayed, there is a far from pretty tale to be told.

The passage of two-and-a-half centuries has blurred the boundaries between history and myth, and thus the accounts of how Tom Lee came to meet so dreadful a fate differ significantly in the detail, although two main versions of the story may be divined. Neither, however, show his character in a good light.

One has it that Lee was a busy man by both night and day: as well as being the village smith, he also served as innkeeper of the Blue Anchor, supplementing his income with the proceeds of highway robbery and burglary. It was whilst engaged in an act of breaking and entering that he was discovered and shot by his victim, who took aim with his pistol and discharged a bullet into the intruder's leg. Now, Lee was a big man, but despite being wounded somehow managed to effect his escape before the householder could reload. It was to Dr Richard Petty whom he repaired, the good doctor removing the ball of lead and staunching the flow of blood, extracting from Lee a confession as to how he had come by his injury. Petty, however, respected the confidence of his patient, and breathed not a word of it. For a while. Indeed, one of the doctor's descendants recently averred that the story told by her family stated that Lee had been shot not during the course of a burglary, but whilst robbing a coach. No matter. The wound and the operation to remove the bullet were one and the same.

It seems that Petty later happened upon Lee, high in his cups at the Angler's Inn in nearby Kilnsey, in vigorous and voluble disputation with a headstrong fellow by the name of Dick Linton. Threatening to tell all of Lee's misdemeanours, Dr Petty hurriedly supped a glass of punch, dropping his glass on the way out, causing the mistress of the house to bid him take care. Fearing the consequences of exposure, Lee rode ahead to lie in waiting for Petty in Grass Wood, and when the latter appeared, fell upon him and bludgeoned him to death. Fleeing the scene, he confided all in his wife, but was overheard by his apprentice. Lee came close to killing the lad so that his secret would be safe, but decided against it, compelling him instead to join him in disposing of the doctor's body. They returned to Grass Wood with a sack, only to find, according to one variant of the tale, the badly injured Petty crawling about in a pathetic and pitiable state. Thus did Lee enjoin his apprentice to deal the fatal blow, thereby securing his silence through his complicity. So ends the first account of the murder.

The other explanation for the killing of Dr Petty is quite different, with it being stated that both Lee and the doctor had on that day been up to Kettlewell, where they placed bets on a cockfight. It was Dr Petty who had the better of it, and having won a considerable sum sank many a celebratory drink in the company of the blacksmith before the two of them, in a great state of inebriation, found themselves in Grass Wood. Seized of a sudden by the desire for his money, Lee turned on his companion and killed him without a second thought.

Whichever variant of the tale you should subscribe to, the account of what then happened to the victim's body is broadly the same. It was moved twice, before finally being taken to Loup Scar, a rocky gorge cut by the River Wharfe close to the village of Burnsall, and there thrown into the water. Lee's wife was with him, the deed being witnessed by two lead miners as they were returning home having taken their fill of drink. The witnesses reported what they had seen, so Tom Lee was arrested. The body, however, could not be found. He was released.

A further two years were to elapse when in 1768 the blacksmith's apprentice confessed, and the murderer of Dr Petty was taken to York assizes and there tried at the castle. He was found guilty and condemned to death by hanging, breathing his last on the twenty-fifth of July that year. Once dead, his body was cut down and returned to his home parish, where it was placed in a gibbet in Grass Wood as a warning to others: break the law in such a fashion, and this too will be your fate. There did it stay until its flesh rotted away, and the bleached bones fell to the ground, leaving only the dead man's spirit to haunt the spot where he once had taken the life of another. His ghost remains there to this day, whereas his smithy is now a gift shop.

The River Wharfe at Loup Scar and Tom Lee's Smithy

Masham's Anglian Crosses and the Church of St Mary

The picturesque market town of Masham, which sits on the River Ure in Wensleydale, is perhaps best known as the home of the Theakston and Black Sheep breweries, but if you should venture here to sample the ale and be inclined towards rooting out historical curiosities, then you could do worse than pay a visit to the parish church of St Mary's. Here, in the churchyard, you will happen upon a rather striking sight: a churchyard high cross of venerable age. Like others of its type, it is richly-carved, but those details which would once have been crisp, and most likely picked out by pigment, have suffered badly from the ravages of weathering. Quite how high this sandstone stump originally stood we cannot be sure, but today it stands at a little in excess of two metres. Of the cross's head, nothing remains.

Historic England dates the cross to the late eighth or early ninth centuries. It has been conjectured that it was raised in dedication to St Wilfrid, who in his various positions as Abbot of Ripon and Bishop of York in the late seventh century was instrumental in the conversion of many of the locals to Christianity. In its form and iconography, the cross is thought to represent a stylistic development of motifs characteristic of early Christian art in the eastern Mediterranean, albeit with a distinctive Anglian twist. Many of the carvings are figurative, depicting Jesus and the Apostles, figures awaiting or undergoing baptism, and possibly the Adoration of the Magi. The Vikings, who raided and burned the town and church round about the turn of the tenth century, would have been able to see the cross in its full glory, but may well not have understood the meaning of the scenes that it portrayed. Was St Mary's standing here at this time, or was it built after the devastation wrought by the Viking attack?

The Stump of Masham's Anglian Cross

The Stump of Masham's Anglian Cross, Southwestern Face

Excavations reveal that Masham's original church was likely founded in the seventh century, and stood in the environs of what is now the town hall. As for the St Mary's that we see today, its fabric is predominantly Norman, albeit with significant additions from the fifteenth century. However, it has also been found to incorporate stonework from before the period of the Conquest.

Inside the church may be seen a large fragment of another Anglian cross – part of a cross-arm – richly decorated with interlacing knotwork. Judging by its size, the shaft that it originally topped must have been of a considerable size. A little to its right may be seen what is described as 'a mid-11th century grave marker, or possibly shaft fragment' which bears upon it a Maltese cross. Alas, the contemporaries who would be able to enlighten us as to the significance of these various artefacts are long since dead. However, the remains of many amongst their number came to light during excavations of the market place in 1988-89, which unearthed 58 skeletons from 'Anglo-Scandinavian Christian burials'. They were radiocarbon dated to 679-1011.

The Tomb of Sir Marmaduke and Lady Magdalan Wyvill
Sir Marmaduke Wyvill, 1st Baronet (1542-1617), became Richmond's first MP in 1584. He seems to have pocketed the seat thanks to the backing of Henry Lord Scrope of Bolton, his mother's uncle, and having done so promptly cried off, a Commons journal entry from 4th December that year noting that he 'is lately fallen very sick and not able to give his attendance on this House till he shall have recovered better health'. Nothing more about his parliamentary involvement is noted, other than that he was once again elected in 1597.

Fragment of an Anglian Cross Arm, Masham

The legal profession appears to have been a draw for him, for he is recorded as having been at Lincoln's Inn in 1560, moving on to complete his education at Cambridge's Pembroke College in 1566. He would later go on to serve as Justice of the Peace for the Riding of North Yorkshire, before embarking upon his distinctly lacklustre parliamentary career.

The only additional surviving documents relating to his worldly activities pertain either to the raw facts of his marriage and burial, or to a variety of transactions concerning property. Not the most colourful of figures, he resided for a time in London before returning to Yorkshire. Created a baronet by James I in 1611, he would die in North Yorkshire in January 1617. His wife, Lady Magdalan, predeceased him in 1613.

The couple's tomb, described disparagingly by a near contemporary as 'cumbrous and costly', was paid for out of the considerable sum of £200 that Sir Marmaduke had set aside to cover the expense of his funeral in his will of August 1614. He is shown in effigy, with his wife recumbent below him. Both stare out at the onlooker from behind bars, as from a prison, begging us to ponder the barebones of their lost lives, whilst beneath them in frozen relief their six surviving sons and two daughters pray for their salvation.

Fashioned from alabaster, the monument is an interesting example of its type. Hints of pigment, particularly on Sir Marmaduke's face, remind us that the effigies would once have been coloured, with its disappearance rendering the couple still more ghostly. The pair are depicted in their very best finery, with Sir Marmaduke aspiring to martial airs in his full plate armour, sword grasped in hand, whereas Lady Magdalan cuts a more peaceful figure, her mantilla drawn up over her head, a prayer book rather than a weapon in her hand. Both adopt recumbent poses typical of the period, propping themselves up on their right arms, their elbows resting upon pillows fashioned, like themselves, from alabaster, which may well have been taken from the ground in Nottinghamshire, or from the renowned works at Chellaston in Derbyshire.

The Tomb of Sir Marmaduke and Lady Magdalan Wyvill

The Remains of Richmond's Franciscan Friary

Grey Friar's Tower, now home to many pigeons as attested to by the prodigious quantity of droppings that spatter the ground below, together with a small section of wall, is all that remains to remind the visitor that once this tranquil Yorkshire town was home to a Franciscan friary. Founded in 1258, the first church to stand on the site was fashioned from timber, but was later rebuilt in stone. The modesty of the early structure was in line with St Francis' teachings on the need for only the most basic of churches and dwellings made of mud and wood, but by the end of the thirteenth century this practice had been largely abandoned, with a general move towards construction in stone observed across England.

By 1386, the complex of buildings had grown to include not only a church, but also a dormitory, a refectory, a guest house, a parlour, and a warden's house. There were also rooms for teaching and washing. Indeed, the friary provided a supply of fresh running water to the townsfolk of Richmond at this time. The tower shown here was built in the fifteenth century, and the warden's house, which stood apart from the main body of the friary, later became the residence of the headmaster of Richmond Grammar School, eventually being incorporated into the present-day Friary Community Hospital.

At the time of its dissolution in January 1539, there were 14 resident brethren including the warden in residence. During excavations in the 1920s and 1990s, human remains were discovered to the south of the church. However, what they did not and could not find was the heart of Ralph Fitz Randal, Lord of Middleham, who granted the initial plot upon which the Friary was built. It is said that this organ was buried in the centre of the church's choir when he died in 1270.

The Ruined Tower of Richmond Friary

The Haunting of Ripley Castle

Remarkably, Ripley Castle has remained in the hands of the same family – the Inglebys – since the manor which preceded it was acquired by Sir Thomas Ingleby (c. 1290-1352) upon his marriage to Edeline Thwenge in 1309 (or 1308 by the old reckoning of dating the beginning of the year from Lady Day – 25th March). It was he who transformed the manor into a castle, and the family lives there to this day.

Over the centuries, the Inglebys have generally remained loyal to the Crown, although their relations with James VI of Scotland and I of England were what might be described as 'complicated'. The king stayed at the castle on his way south to claim the English throne after the death of Elizabeth I in 1603, but only two years later the Inglebys had turned against the new monarch and were heavily complicit in the Gunpowder Plot. However, whereas some nine of the conspirators were either closely related to the family, or were close associates, both Sir William Ingleby and his son were cleared of charges. Indeed, the Inglebys' Catholic sympathies were longstanding, with one family member, named Francis Ingleby, having become a Catholic priest. For this he was hanged, drawn and quartered in York in 1586. However, Sir William Ingleby, who proved a staunch supporter of the Royalist cause during the Civil War, fled from Marston Moor to cower in the castle's priest hole as Cromwell himself elected to stay at his home for the night. Sir William's sister, Jane, reputedly stalled the future Lord Protector by confronting him with a pistol whilst her brother dashed to his place of concealment. He was not found.

The alleged haunting of the castle, however, would seem to involve none of the above characters. The ghostly activity, which some have characterised as being akin to that of a poltergeist, is attributed to the figure of Lady Alicia Ingilby and her two children who died at a tender age during the 1870s. A number of witnesses have allegedly seen her mournful ghost walking straight through a locked door as she makes her way to her children's bedrooms. It is claimed that the unblocking of a chimney in the Tower Room in the middle of the last century prompted an outburst of poltergeist activity, with furniture being moved and pictures turned backwards. Its most recent alleged flurry took place in 2017 when a number of silver Georgian candlesticks 'reappeared' having vanished three years earlier. They came to light in a bag in the castle's strong room just after the family had received an insurance payment for their 'theft'. The Ingilbys were quite emphatic that they had searched that very room from top to bottom on three separate occasions and yet not found them. What had happened to them in the interim? I'll leave you to be the judge. And if you should ever see anything unsettling at Ripley Castle and repair to the local pub – the Boar's Head – to soothe your nerves, be warned: the pub is also said to be haunted.

Ripley and the Legend of the Ingilby Boar

The North Yorkshire village of Ripley, formerly in Yorkshire's historic West Riding, is a pleasant little place that's certainly worth a visit should you find yourself in the area. Being an estate village, its layout and architecture possess all of the aesthetic appeal that you might expect, and the Ingilby family still resides at its castle. As for its parish church, All Saints, it too is full of historical interest. However, before you step inside you may notice a curious squat structure of stone into which is slotted a wooden crucifix: Ripley's 'Weeping Cross'. Around its base are a number of recesses – knee holes – carved into the stone so that pilgrims and penitents might kneel at the cross to pray. It is, so the notice claims, the only remaining cross of its type in England, although much of its fabric has been lost leaving just this stump.

There is an interesting legend attached to the Ingilby family which accounts for how Thomas de Ingilby came to acquire a knighthood. Whereas the notice in the church states that Sir Thomas was born in 1290 and died in 1369, his life may not have been quite as lengthy as it suggests, for his identity may have been confused with that of his father, also named Thomas, who in other sources is said to have been born in 1290. It may therefore be the case that the Thomas in this story lived from 1310 to 1369.

Thomas de Ingilby gained his favour through a singular act that may have saved the life of Edward III. One day, when the king was visiting the area, it was decided that there should be a hunt in the royal forest of Knaresborough, and Ingilby duly accompanied his sovereign as part of the hunting party. At that time, it would seem, wild boar were still to be found, and it was one such beast which having been wounded by Edward's spear turned upon the king and charged his mount. The horse threw the monarch to the ground, and in that instant when the enraged boar looked about to wreak its revenge upon its tormentor, Thomas slew it and saved Edward's life. For this deed he was duly knighted, with the boar's head being granted as the Ingilby crest. The grateful king also gave the family the right to hold a market and a horse fair in the village.

The boar may be seen represented atop the carved helm upon which the head of Thomas's effigy rests. It is an odd-looking creature with a curiously elongated head of somewhat bovine appearance. That said, the effigies of Sir Thomas and his wife, Edeline, despite having suffered significant damage over the centuries, are carefully carved and well executed. The tomb was originally located in an earlier building located about half a mile away that owing to subsidence became known as the 'Sinking Chapel'. The famous boar also makes an appearance on the funeral pennants of Sir William Ingleby (1546-1617) which hang from the ceiling of the Ingleby Chapel, in which his armoured effigy may be seen resting upon a chest tomb. It would seem, however, that he would not be allowed to rest in peace, for when Cromwell and his men made themselves uninvited guests at the neighbouring Ripley Castle after their victory at Marston Moor, they also paid a visit to the church. In their opinion, something needed to be added to Sir William's glowing epitaph, for below the cartouche in which it was inscribed they carved the words, 'NO POMPE, NOR PRIDE. LET GOD BE HONORED.' This was their verdict on the deceased Catholic sympathiser.

Venturing back out into the village you will find another representation of the Ingilby Boar in the form of a carving that graces a commemorative drinking fountain gifted to the village in 1907, as well as the Boar's Head Inn named in its honour.

Tomb of Thomas de Ingilby and His Wife

The boar atop his sculpted helm, rather resembling a calf

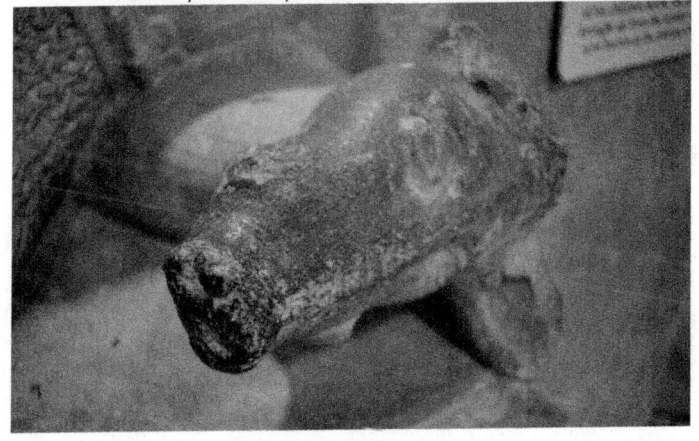

Pennants of Sir William Ingleby (1546-1617)

Parliamentarian Graffiti on Sir William Ingleby's Tomb

Drinking Fountain, Ripley

Lord Dacre's Tomb, Saxton

It has to be said that this chest tomb looks nothing out of the ordinary. Quite unremarkable, in fact, although quite an unusual tale has come to be attached to it. With its inscription long since weathered away, and its heraldic device now only faintly discernible, we do at least know who lies buried here: Ralph, or Ranulph, Lord Dacre of Gilsland (or Gillesland in its archaic spelling). And here he has lain for more than 560 years, having fallen for the Lancastrian cause at the Battle of Towton.

Palm Sunday, which fell on 29 March 1461, was a bitter day indeed. In driving sleet and snow, two armies of Englishmen faced each other on the open field of nearby Towton. Although the numbers are disputed, it is believed that this was the largest battle ever fought on English soil, with modern estimates claiming the total of the opposing armies to have numbered somewhere in the region of 50,000-65,000 men. If so, perhaps 2% of the English population here met under arms. Contemporary accounts place the death toll at up to 38,000, but this is not regarded as overly credible. Lower figures of around 9,000-13,500 may be nearer the mark, but these are horrifying enough. The blood that flood would dye the waters of the neighbouring Cock Beck a lurid red, and leave a permanent stain upon history.

The Lancastrian rout saw a stampede down through what would later come to be known as the 'Bloody Meadow', towards the swollen waters of the beck. How tranquil it looks today, but not then. Quite how many fell and drowned, weighed down by their armour and trampled underfoot by their desperate comrades and pursuers, we cannot say with any certainty. But the number of dead and dying was such that they came to choke the swollen watercourse, forming bridges of bodies over which the later fugitives would clamber.

Lord Dacre, it is averred, was killed by an archer positioned in the witch's tree – an elder – known in the local dialect as a 'bur tree'. The boy, whose father had been slain earlier that day by Dacre, loosed his arrow at his target when the latter had 'unclasped his helmet' to take a sip of wine.

After the battle his body was taken to nearby Saxton, and there it is said to have been buried. Nothing particularly unusual about that, you might think, although it is claimed that his corpse was not laid in the earth in the usual manner, but mounted on his dead horse. A most unusual, and impractical, arrangement. Could this really be true? Whatever the case, a far more modern memorial of stone now sits next to it, the inscription on one of its faces declaring: 'Here lie the remains of unknown soldiers found at Towton Hall 1996 and killed at the Battle of Towton Palm Sunday 19th March 1461.' Did any of these men fight on Lord Dacre's side, or against him? They now rest together for eternity, or until their remains are once more disturbed by human hand.

St Mary's Church and the Lost Village of South Cowton

Although the parish of South Cowton still exists, the village that once bore this name is now all but erased, leaving little more to suggest its presence than the Church of St Mary and South Cowton Castle. If, therefore, you should be tempted to seek out what you see in these pictures, be warned: it is far from easy to find. The church itself is little frequented, situated as it is at the end of a rough farm track, and maintained by the Churches Conservation Trust. Anyone tempted to drive its length should be aware that doing so might incur the loss of their exhaust.

Both church and castle date from the time of the Wars of the Roses, with the structure of St Mary's being described as aptly 'fortress-like'. It is a pretty enough building, but it was the lure of the three alabaster effigies situated within that had drawn me here. They are fine examples of their type, ripped from where they once rested, the two ladies stacked on a rack like corpses in some morgue. It is a pity that all three figures are placed hard by the church walls, for this prevents the visitor from fully appreciating their artistry, and renders photography awkward. Their removal from the now-vanished tombs that they once adorned makes the definite identification of these individuals impossible, although it has been suggested that the knight may be either Sir Richard Boynton, who died before 1485, or Sir Richard Conyers (1425-1502?). It is the second of these men who in 1470 oversaw the building of the castle, which nowadays is a private farmhouse. If the carving indeed represents Conyers, which is thought more probable, then one of the female effigies will likely represent his wife, Alice Wycliffe. As to whichever of the two is not Alice, there are no agreed suggestions as to her identity.

It is thought likely that the three pieces were carved at Chellaston in Derbyshire, which was renowned for the creation of such works at this time. Indeed, in both style and the quality of the carving employed, this trio bring to mind some stunningly well-preserved examples at Norbury in Derbyshire. Here at South Cowton, the details of both dress and armour are particularly fine, and traces of pigment persist on the female figures, providing a suggestion as to their original colourful appearance. If you should find yourself in this part of North Yorkshire, and are confident of your navigational abilities, then I would certainly recommend dropping in to visit these three, whoever they may be.

Mediaeval Effigies, St Mary's Church, South Cowton

Effigy of Unknown Knight, St Mary's Church, South Cowton

Effigy of Unknown Lady, St Mary's Church, South Cowton

Stainmoor's Headless Horsewoman

Such is the fickle nature of administrative boundaries that what was once historically in one county now often finds itself in another. And in the case of Stainmore, or Stainmoor as once it was spelt, we find three counties, at one time or another, vying claim to stretches of that bleak tract of land: County Durham, North Yorkshire, and Cumbria. And whereas it is in contemporary Cumbria that the parish itself lies, a portion of this moorland once belonged to the North Riding of Yorkshire, and as the following story was recounted in a publication detailing the folklore of that region, it is told here. It is a grim and colourful tale, with a most unchivalrous outcome. And it is said to have taken place the best part of a thousand years ago, not so long after the Norman Conquest.

Two rival parties were in the habit of hunting boar upon the moor, one Norman, and one Saxon. On those occasions when the two met, they would come to blows, for there was no love to be had between them. However, the Norman Fitz-Barnard had a beautiful daughter of twenty years of age who once went hunting in the company of her father's retainers. Surprised by the rival party of a local Saxon chieftain, she and a number of her companions were captured and taken prisoner, for the chieftain, much taken with her charms, was determined to make her his wife. She, however, remained immune to his blandishments, despite his repeated attempts to woo her.

After some time, a plan was hatched and she was successfully sprung from captivity. As she and her rescuers made their way across the moor towards the safety of home, the Saxon chieftain bore down upon her with his men, their charge being so fierce that her guard were overcome. The enraged Saxon, unwilling to yield her to any other man, took her head off with a single swipe of his sword. And thus was born, so it was said, a terrible sight that would haunt this place down the centuries: a headless horsewoman galloping at midnight upon the moor, accompanied by strange sights and sounds of men in their roaring tumult.

The Church of St John the Baptist, Stanwick

Now cared for by the Churches Conservation Trust, St John's contains much of interest for the visitor beyond the stunningly carved effigies that grace the Smithson tomb. The church itself is set within the bounds of the massive Iron Age complex of earthworks known as Stanwick Camp, conjectured to have been the site of the 'capital' of the Brigantes during the reign of their queen, Cartimandua, during the First Century AD.

The date of the church's foundation is lost, and whereas the present structure dates from the thirteenth century, it is plain from the 'beak heads' and fragments of grave slabs and carved stones from the preceding two centuries set into the wall of its porch, that an earlier building once stood here. Then there is the testimony of the remains of two elaborately-carved pre-Conquest crosses – one standing in the churchyard, and another inside the church. The former is the less impressive of the two, a single short stump set in a modern base, the decoration on its narrow sides surviving better than whatever once graced its two broader faces. It is covered in white, grey, green, and mustard-hued lichen, topped with dainty cushions of moss. The cross beneath the tower, however, readily arrests the eye and excites curiosity. Comprised of three main fragments, once again set within a modern base, its carvings are quite clear, and besides the usual interlaced motifs characteristic of a piece of its period, it boasts a beast or two, as well as a symbol described in the church literature as a "Jellinge' hart, and hound ribbon ornamentation.' It is thought to date from either the ninth or tenth centuries, a time when Stanwick lay within the northernmost bounds of the Danelaw.

Elsewhere in St John's may be seen three badly weathered mediaeval stone effigies, the identities of those whom they commemorate now lost. Propped up on its side next to the outside of its wall is an empty stone sarcophagus with a clearly carved recess for the head, and set into the outer face of the churchyard wall is a well, protected beneath the canopy of a gothic arch. The source of this well – a spring – is clearly marked by the presence of a small stone cell sitting in the middle of a field about 150 metres from the church. This, like the decorative structure housing the well itself, was built for the Duke of Northumberland during the nineteenth century.

The Church of St John the Baptist, Stanwick

The Smithson Tomb
This magnificent monument is the most impressive artwork housed within Stanwick's parish church, and possesses a link, of sorts, to one of the United States' most famous cultural establishments: the Smithsonian Institution. The clue, unsurprisingly, is in the name of the tomb, although the pair of Smithsons buried here was in no way directly

connected to its foundation. It was named in honour of their descendant, the British scientist James Smithson (1765-1829). Having no children, this latter Smithson left his money to his nephew Henry Hungerford, who when he also died childless in 1835 bequeathed his fortune to the US government with the instruction that it should be used 'for the increase and diffusion of knowledge among men.' This generous bequest took the form of 105 sacks of gold sovereigns, totalling 104,960 coins.

Returning to the tomb, this particularly fine pair of effigies, thought to have been carved by William Stanton, commemorates the lives of Sir Hugh Smithson (1598-1670) and his wife Dorothy. Like many men of his time, Sir Hugh was to see his fortunes wax and wane and wax again in line with the turbulent political changes of his era. Being a Royalist, he remained loyal to Charles II during his period of exile, and by refusing to pledge allegiance to, and collaborate with, the Commonwealth regime eventually had his estate sequestered. With the Restoration his estates were restored, the grateful king granting him an augmented coat of arms in recognition of his loyalty and service.

Although Sir Hugh purchased the manor of Stanwick in 1638, he spent much of his time elsewhere, for he also possessed holdings in Suffolk, Middlesex and Yorkshire's East Riding. His home when he died was far away at Tottenham High Cross. Stanwick, however, must have possessed a special place in his heart, for this is where he chose to be laid to rest.

The Smithson Tomb, St John the Baptist, Stanwick

Effigy of Sir Hugh Smithson (1598-1670)

Effigy of Dorothy Smithson (c. 1607-1692)

Stanwick Iron Age Fortifications

The scale of the area enclosed by Stanwick's Iron Age encampment is vast, totalling some 300 hectares, which dwarfs the 19 hectares of Dorset's better known iconic hillfort from this period, Maiden Castle. However, whereas Maiden Castle's banks and ditches, which take advantage of a natural hill, retain much of their stature and are plain to the eye, those at Stanwick have not survived so well, although its earthen banks, which stretch some 6.4 kilometres, remain impressive in places. The settlement, or oppidum, that once stood in this area of North Yorkshire, is believed to have been the power centre of the Brigantes. It is thought that it would have provided a home to their first-century queen, Cartimandua, who allied herself with the occupying Romans. In AD 51, Caratacus, a defiant chieftain of the Catuvellauni tribe who resisted Roman rule, sought sanctuary amongst the Brigantes, but Cartimandua denied him her protection, binding him in chains and handing him over to the Romans instead.

Excavations at the site reveal that activity at Stanwick was already waning towards the end of the first century as, presumably, the local population became increasingly Romanised and gravitated towards the new, and more comfortable, Roman settlements. One of the better preserved sections of bank and ditch, excavated by a team led by Sir Mortimer Wheeler in 1951-52, is now covered by trees and topped by a footpath, providing a short walk during which the visitor can try to visualise how once this defensive structure might have appeared. It presents a challenging task to the imagination.

Ditch and Rampart at Stanwick Camp

In 1845 a hoard of 140 metal artefacts was unearthed at Melsonby about half a mile from the fortifications. These included a striking stylised horse-head mask fashioned from bronze, and four sets of horse harness for chariots. It has been conjectured, owing to the lack of a firm provenance, that the so-called 'Meyrick Helmet', held in the British Museum, was discovered as part of the Stanwick Hoard. It was donated to the museum in 1872, having earlier been part of Sir Samuel Rush Meyrick's (1783-1848) collection of arms and armour. Its design is interesting insofar as its overall form appears to have been modelled upon a Roman auxiliary helmet, and would originally have sported a plume and cheekpieces. The neck guard, however, possesses a distinctive La Tène style decoration, and would once have been decorated with red glass enamel studs. This syncretistic style begs the question as to whether it might have been the property of a British auxiliary fighting alongside the Romans, or whether the helmet was simply inspired by Roman designs and belonged to a member of the Brigantes tribe fighting against the Romans.

The 'Meyrick Helmet': Part of the Stanwick Hoard?

The Mystery of Trow Ghyll

Trow Ghyll makes for a dramatic, and at times, forbidding sight. With its towering walls and boulder-strewn floor, it often, particularly on a winter's day, presents itself in a dismal and oppressive light, the overhanging trees clutching at the clifftops threatening to tumble down upon those who pass below. It is a passage familiar to many walkers who follow the trail from the village of Clapham towards the flat-topped summit of Ingleborough, but few of them will perhaps be familiar with the unusual story that I am about to recount. It possesses, for once, nothing relating to the supernatural, although its oddity is sufficient to place it well beyond the ambit of everyday experience. And it remains, just about, within the realm of living memory.

Being limestone country, the area is riddled with caverns, not least of which is the mighty Gaping Gill, the largest known cave in the country. And it was thanks to the enquiring nature of two potholers in search of new subterranean adventures that a most intriguing, if somewhat gruesome, discovery was made. The two friends – Jim Leach and Harold Burgess – were not local to the area, but both townsmen. One of them was from Blackburn, the other from Leeds, and they discovered a new cave some 900 yards or so distant from Trow Ghyll. And in this cave, on 24 August 1947, they found something altogether unexpected: a human skeleton, an unsettling discovery immortalised in the name chosen for the cave: 'Body Pot'.

The remains came to light as the two men were removing stones to enlarge the entrance, its presence announced by the sight of a pair of shoes, some ten feet into the pothole. Looking round, Mr Leach then saw a skull and the body partially obscured by a large stone. Only a few scraps of flesh remained. Close to the body was a bottle containing a white powder. The police were duly called in, and the following day photographs were taken before the remains and personal effects were taken to Skipton and Wakefield respectively. Signs of foul play were absent, with the post-mortem ascertaining that the remains belonged to a man in his twenties who had been dead for anywhere between two and six years. Although his clothes were in a poor state, the manner and style of his dress were readily ascertained, but it was not his attire that excited interest, but rather the discovery of sodium cyanide in the bottle found with the body. Moreover, an unused ampule containing the same substance was also found. All of the coins the man had been carrying dated from before 1940; a top from a mineral water bottle was from a make not introduced until that year, and was known to be a brand of refreshment used in certain hotels in neighbouring Lancashire and Ingleton. Many other personal effects were also found, but it was the sodium cyanide that excited the most interest. Why was he carrying it? What purpose could it possibly have served? Had he committed suicide using some of the substance in the bottle? It was held to be a possibility, for the bottle was not full.

An attempt was made to match the skeleton to a list of missing people, but many of them proved to be either alive, or to bear no resemblance to the remains. Four possible matches could not be eliminated, but neither could they be confirmed. Whereas the bottle of sodium cyanide could potentially be explained away as having been used as rat poison, the existence of the ampule containing this same poison could not. The latter was of a type issued to spies so that they might use it to commit suicide should they be captured. Indeed, it is thought that Hermann Göring escaped his death sentence at Nuremberg by using just such a means. A local legal historian, named A.W.B. Simpson, thus suggested that the remains were those of a German agent. However, extensive analysis of German intelligence documents during the post-war period failed to bring to light any Nazi agents sent to Britain during the Second World War who had not already been accounted for. So, who was the man found in Body Pot? And if he was a spy, what was he doing in the Yorkshire Dales, far away from airfields, military bases, and centres of production of materiel? It is a mystery to which a solution may never be found.

The Marmion Tower, West Tanfield

A remnant of a once larger structure it may be, but a most appealing one at that. True, it lacks a roof or any other convenience that would render it habitable, but its aesthetic allure is considerable. Marmion Tower, raised in the fifteenth century, once served as the gatehouse to Tanfield Castle, which, it would seem, did not thrive. In 1314, John Marmion received a licence to crenellate his home in West

Tanfield, with the manor being duly fortified and transformed into a modest castle, of which no trace remains other than the tower seen here which was built at a much later date by Sir Henry Fitzhugh.

By the time that Tudor antiquary John Leland visited the village in around 1540, it was the tower rather than the manor that he thought worthy of greater remark: 'The castle of Tanfeld, or rather as it is now, a mean manor place, stands hard on the [bank] of [the] Ure, where I saw no notable building but a fair towered gatehouse and a hall of squared stone.'

When the last of the Fitzhughs died, the ownership of the manor passed to William Parr, brother of his rather more famous sister, Catherine, and in 1571, it passed into a pair of even more famous and influential hands: those of Elizabeth I's chief adviser, William Cecil, Lord Burghley.

At some point, West Tanfield Castle was dismantled, with its materials being carted off to be reused in nearby structures owned by prominent local families in Snape and Kirklington.

Marmion Tower is open to visitors, and if you are steady of foot and not faint of heart, you may ascend its somewhat perilous spiral staircase to the first floor and gaze out from its striking oriel window. Views may also be had of the adjacent River Ure. If you should choose to ascend the steps further, you will find that they abruptly terminate having taken you nowhere but upwards, with the second floor being, quite rightly, sealed off, as its physical floor vanished long ago. A number of the steps also rest upon a perilously weathered central support that has lost at least half of its mass, which is enough to induce a sense of vertigo in the steadiest of heads. I didn't notice its state until I was making my way back down. Take care where you place your foot.

The Marmion Tower, West Tanfield

The Church of St Nicholas, West Tanfield

Despite a sweeping restoration of the church's interior in 1859 that removed much of its mediaeval heritage, not everything from that earlier period was lost. Although it dates from the cusp of the twelfth and thirteenth centuries, its basic structure took on its present shape in the fifteenth. That it has been a holy site since long before is demonstrated by the presence of a heavily-weathered Anglian cross fragment which stands in the graveyard. Even so, the intricacy of its original decorative scheme may still be discerned.

Inside St Nicholas's may be seen a number of mediaeval effigies resting upon a series of chest tombs laid out along the wall of the north aisle. None of these are in a particularly good state of preservation, the stone of two of them having crumbled away in places. Not all of the identities of the individuals whom these memorials commemorate are known, although one is believed to be Sir William Marmion who died in 1275. Three ladies are represented, including two from the fourteenth century. It is the oldest of them – the figure of a cross-legged knight, helmeted, carrying a shield and dressed in mail – that is the least damaged of the set, despite having been carved in around 1250. There is, however, one further tomb here that is far more impressive, which belongs to Sir John and Lady Elizabeth Marmion.

A Memorial to the Last Roundhead

So many things are so easily overlooked. How many, after all, pause in their travels to explore the small and picturesque village of West Tanfield, situated on the River Ure in North Yorkshire? And of those, how many trouble themselves to venture beyond its agreeable hostelries to the Church of St Nicholas, and there look down to the base of the porch and notice this tantalising inscription:

Here lyeth the body of Ralph Bourn. Born Anno 1615 and died in 1728.

Of Ralph, no more is said. The facts of his life, besides this bald statement of his lengthy earthly sojourn, appear unknown. And what does the 'Here lyeth' mean? Was he literally buried in the church porch, or beneath the fabric of its stones? I do not know. In any era, to survive to the age of 113 is quite exceptional, but in Ralph's time this would have been wondrous. There are others from early modern England who claimed to have lived to an even greater age, but their stories will have to wait until another day.

After a little digging, however, I did manage to exhume something, albeit not much, relating to the conduct of Ralph's long life. In the third volume of J. and J.B. Burke's *Heraldic Illustrations*, it is noted that this particular Ralph Bourn 'is said to have been the last surviving soldier, who had served in the army of Cromwell.' It is sobering to think that he lived for a little over three quarters of a century after Worcester. And yet, it would seem that the last pair of eyes belonging to a combatant in England's Civil War were not his, but those of one of two men who fought on the other side at Edgehill in 1642: William Walker (1613-1736) of Ribchester in Lancashire, and William Hiseland (1620-1733) from Wiltshire. Walker's claimed age of 122 has, unsurprisingly, been disputed, with Hiseland's seen as much more credible.

The lack of certainty regarding the identity of England's last survivor from this conflict provided an interesting premise for historical author Jemahl Evans, who was thus prompted to write his novel *The Last Roundhead*. Its fictitious protagonist – Blandford Candy – is an irascible chap. Quite what, if anything, he would have had in common with the character of Ralph Bourn, we shall likely never know.

Inscription commemorating the 'Last Roundhead', Ralph Bourn

The Marmion Tower and the Church of St Nicholas

Anglian Cross Shaft, West Tanfield

The Tomb of Sir John and Lady Elizabeth Marmion
The two effigies that grace the tomb of this noble couple are exceptionally fine. Fashioned from Derbyshire alabaster, likely taken from the ground at Chellaston, it is a material that allowed the sculptor to render in fine detail the armour and costume of the time. Some damage has been incurred down the ages. Sir John has lost both hands, whereas Lady Elizabeth's fingers have been broken away. The two figures have also been incised with graffiti.

Sir John was to die whilst fighting in Spain in 1387 under John of Gaunt in his unsuccessful attempt of April to June of that year to unseat the Castilian king and claim the throne for himself. Lady Elizabeth remained at home, where it is thought she may have lived in the Marmion Tower, the shell of which stills stands close to the church in which she is buried. She survived her husband by a number of years, passing away in 1400, although the couple left no children.

The tomb is notable also for its wrought-iron 'hearse', which the church description avers 'to be the only one of its kind in England.' That said, a hearse of wrought iron, originally from Lincolnshire, is held in the collections of the Victoria and Albert Museum. The example here at West Tanfield in North Yorkshire is an odd-looking contraption, possessing a number of 'prickets' for the holding of candles that would have been lit on certain special occasions. The detail of Sir John's plate armour and chainmail is captured particularly well, and about his neck may be seen a Lancastrian collar. Who carved these effigies I do not know, although the pains taken by the mason, or masons, who worked upon them would have been considerable.

Effigies of Sir John and Lady Elizabeth Marmion

Effigy of Sir John Marmion

Sir John Marmion's Helm in Alabaster

Head of Lady Elizabeth Marmion supported by Angels

Rutland
Echoes of North Luffenham's Explosive Past

Not so long ago, the Rutland village of North Luffenham resounded to the roar of jet engines from the planes of its former RAF base, but several centuries earlier it was the roar of cannon and the crack of musket fire that here rent the air. In 1642, some 1300 Parliamentarian troops came to take North Luffenham Hall, defended by 200 Royalists under Henry Noel. Despite the disparity in numbers, Noel's force resisted the attackers, even calling into service a butter churn which they transformed into a makeshift cannon. It fired but the once, exploding and wounding the men who had fired it. Ultimately, the besiegers had the better of it, and having plundered the hall and neighbouring church alike, smashed the latter's windows and defaced a statue of Noel's wife, marched off in triumph, taking with them the Royalist commander who died shortly afterwards in London.

As if this were not enough explosive action for such a quiet village, it also possesses associations with Sir Everard Digby, one of the frustrated gunpowder plotters who sought to blow up King James I at the opening of Parliament in 1605. On 30 January 1606 he met a grisly end: having been found guilty of treason, he was hanged, drawn and quartered. His wife and two young sons were amongst the onlookers who bore witness to his ignoble fate. As the executioner held up the dying man's heart before the crowd declaring it to be that of a traitor, Digby is reported to have somehow summoned up sufficient energy to cry out his indignant denial.

Returning to North Luffenham, its former manor, which today bears the name of North Luffenham Hall (the original hall which was besieged during the Civil War was demolished in 1806, the village primary school now occupying its site), belonged to the Digby family. And if the stories are to be believed, Sir Everard on occasion makes a return to this former residence. A sighting is said to have taken place in 1957, although quite how the witness came to recognise him is not made clear; it would seem unlikely that he introduced himself. Even on a hot day, the house's parlour is said to possess 'freezing cold pockets', but being a resident of an old house myself (albeit of very modest dimensions), with thick stone walls and a living room which is colder in summer than in winter owing to the lack of a fire in the warmer season, I do not find the presence of such 'pockets' a surprise. They would seem to be a perfectly natural phenomenon. However, as with many ghosts of famous historical personages, Sir Digby Everard is also said to make post-mortem appearances elsewhere, this time in association with a coach driven by a headless driver, which rattles along the road to Halstead from his childhood home at Tilton-on-the-Hill in Leicestershire.

Somerset
Bladud: Bath's Legendary Founder

Bath may be best known for the elegance of its Georgian architecture and its Roman baths, but its origins, like those of most historical cities, are obscure. According to Geoffrey of Monmouth, it was founded by Bladud, a king of the Britons who supposedly reigned during the ninth century BC. As with much of the content of Geoffrey's *Historia regum Britanniae* (The History of the Kings of Britain), his account of Bladud and his life is rather fanciful, and is more myth than history. That said, it makes for an entertaining tale.

The story goes that Bladud, although of royal blood, was shunned and denied his liberty because he had contracted leprosy. Having managed to escape, he secured work as a swineherd, and it was whilst minding his pigs that he noticed that they indulged in a certain curious behaviour: whenever the weather was cold they would wander off to wallow in a particular patch of black mud. Examining this, he found it to be warm. He also discovered that it appeared to protect the pigs from ailments of the skin, and thus elected to follow their example and immersed himself in their wallow. To his delight, he soon found himself cured of leprosy. When he became king, he founded the city around its miraculous hot spring. A tidy origin myth.

Bladud was also held to have indulged in black magic, and to have attempted to fly by means of a pair of artificial wings. Like Icarus, it was this early experiment with flight that is said to have caused his mortal demise. Thanks to Shakespeare, however, it is his son who is better known to us: King Lear.

Bladud exerted a certain fascination for one of Georgian Bath's most celebrated architects – John Wood – who wrote of him in his work *The Essay towards a description of Bath*. He also propagated the rather fanciful notion that Bladud was responsible for the construction of stone circles such as Stanton Drew, and thus thought highly of him, for Wood was also a keen exponent of the druidic revival, claiming Bladud as an erstwhile practitioner of druidism. Wood's surveys of Stonehenge and Stanton Drew are even today held in high regard for their accuracy, whereas his interpretation of their origins and purpose have not withstood the test of time so well.

The Pulteney Bridge, Bath

Bishops Lydeard: its Church and a Devilish Visitation

The Church of St Mary's in Bishops Lydeard is an imposing affair built from the red sandstone of the neighbouring Quantock Hills. Its great tower was built at the close of the fifteenth century, and most of the current structure of the church dates from that century and the one that preceded it. However, the first mention of a church on the site dates from

1239, and it is highly likely that such a building had stood here for many years before.

The church's interior is spacious, and its well-preserved painted rood screen dating from the early sixteenth century is a sight to behold. If you are interested in carved bench ends, then you will not be disappointed, as the church hosts a varied and unique selection. Dating from the early sixteenth century, they include familiar motifs such as a green man and a pelican (which here, as in most churches, only resembles a pelican insofar as it possesses wings and feathers) feeding its young with blood from its breast. Of greater originality and interest are those showing a ship; a windmill; a stag; and a man with rather springy and buoyant hair grasping two great vines or trunks. Unusually, all of these carvings are set against painted backgrounds of red and blue, with at least two of these featuring shields painted gold.

The Jacobean pulpit is richly carved and ornate, and like the bench ends is painted in blue, red and gold. Likewise, its fifteenth-century octagonal font boasts an array of decorative carving, although none of it is coloured. One other curiosity housed in St Mary's that merits a look is a royal charter of Edward I, complete with its large seal which dates from 1291. It may be translated as: 'To Robert [Burnell] bishop of Bath and Wells, granting a weekly market on Mondays at his manor of Bishops Lydeard, a fair on the Vigil, Day, Morrow and 3 days following (6 days) of the Feast of the Nativity of the Blessed Virgin Mary, and another fair on the Vigil, Day, Morrow, and 3 days following, of the Feast of the Annunciation of the Blessed Virgin Mary.'

In the churchyard may be seen the remains of two large mediaeval crosses, one dating from the fourteenth century and carved with the twelve apostles about its base, the other having been the village cross which was moved to its present position during the Victorian period.

Somewhere not so far from the church is a well with a curious name and a similarly curious story, but I failed to happen upon it during my brief visit. It is known as the Devil's Whispering Well. As to how it came to acquire such a name, and when, that is a matter of some obscurity, although an article published in the *Local Notes and Queries of the Somerset Herald* on 31st August 1935 purports to provide an explanation. The correspondent reported that when he was a child he remembers his grandmother telling him that the Devil would repeatedly appear next to a well in the village near to where a group of men were engaged in building work. Unlike in many stories involving the Devil, he did not on this occasion appear interested in bargaining with any of the men for their souls, or offer anything by way of a tempting inducement to surrender them. Still, his presence proved unwelcome, and so discomfited were they by his loitering and their being watched over by none other than Old Nick himself, that they took themselves off to the local clergyman, and begged that he might offer them some advice as to how to banish their unbidden companion.

Happy to volunteer his services, the vicar asked when they thought the Devil would next appear, and having received an answer duly joined them at the allotted hour. Up popped the Devil, looking for all the world like an ordinary chap but for one rather telling characteristic: his cloven hoof. The cleric here advanced uttering the words, 'In the name of the father, the son and the Holy Ghost, why troublest thou me?' Satan offered no reply, and simply faded from view. 'Wall him in', said the clergyman, and so the workmen built a wall about that spot where there diabolical visitant had appeared. He was never to trouble them again.

St Mary's Church, Bishops Lydeard

Part of Rood Screen, St Mary's Church, Bishops Lydeard

Bench End, St Mary's Church, Bishops Lydeard

Bench End, St Mary's Church, Bishops Lydeard

Pulpit, St Mary's Church, Bishops Lydeard

Bruton's Bramble Briar and Bullbeggar of Creech Hill

The Somerset town of Bruton has acquired a certain vogue of late. Might it be said to be in Somerset, but no longer of Somerset? So some have claimed, given the recent influx of well-heeled Londoners such as former Chancellor George Osborne, together with a number of very wealthy folk from elsewhere. However, as it is somewhere with which I have only a passing acquaintance, you may well be better placed to pass comment on the town's present character than I.

The most well-known piece of folklore associated with Bruton concerns a traditional murder ballad, which has appeared under a number of names and in a number of guises, with titles including *In Bruton Town*, *The Merchant's Daughter*, and, most evocatively, *The Bramble Briar*. Its theme, as you might guess, is one of doomed love, with the lovers in question being a servant and his mistress who resolved that they should marry. It was not to be.

The young lady in question had two brothers who, getting wind of the pair's intentions, devised a scheme to dispose of her lowly suitor. They thus murdered him whilst hunting in the woods, concealing his body in a thicket of brambles, later telling tell their sister that the servant had been 'lost'. And yet, she dreamt that night, and in her dreaming she saw the fearful sight of her dead and bloodied lover. The next day she walked out, and in her rambling through the woods happened upon the thicket and discovered the dead man. Upon his cold lips she planted a kiss. This did not, however, revive him, and for three days she sat with the corpse. When she returned home she accused her brothers of murder, and in one version of the song she brings with her the dead man's head which she has placed in a jar. In essence, the ballad has been deigned to be a retelling of Bocaccio's fourteenth-century tale 'Isabella and the Pot of Basil'.

Not so far from Bruton stands Creech Hill, which boasts a ghost that goes by the singular name of 'Bullbeggar'. Here, in the 1880s, two bodies were discovered during quarrying, and it was shortly after they came to light that the haunting began. The ghost manifested itself in a number of different ways, including a 'black uncanny shape' and disembodied footsteps. On another occasion it took the rather more definite form of a figure which laid itself out upon the road. On his way home late one night, a farmer paused to help a stranger, only to find that the figure rose from the carriageway and repaid his kindness by pursuing him to his door. It was only when his family came to his assistance that his tormentor bounded away with a maniacal laugh. The folklorist Katharine Briggs conjectures that Bullbeggar may be a variation upon the theme of the black dog, albeit one that 'goes on its hind legs'. She notes that there is a tale of a Bruton man who did battle with the spirit for the length of a whole night. Having nothing to defend himself beyond a length of hazel, there was no let-up in this assault until his assailant promptly vanished at cockcrow. In another version of this story, it is a staff of ash that he employs in his defence. When was Bullbeggar last sighted? Someone will know.

Bruton High Street

St Mary's Church, Bruton: Tombs and Curiosities
This is undoubtedly a very fine church, with origins reaching back to the seventh century when it was founded by King Ine of Wessex (reigned 689-726). Rather unusually for a man of such political significance, whom Stenton dubbed the strongest Saxon king of his time, Ine relinquished his throne so that he might die at Rome. However, nothing of this original structure remains, and what is seen today dates largely from the fourteenth to early sixteenth centuries.

Its most notable tomb belongs to Sir Maurice Berkeley and his two wives. The brass plaque appended to this monument states that he was born in around 1506, and died in 1580, although the latter date may be recorded as 1581 if the then custom of reckoning the New Year from Lady Day (25th March) is discounted. His first wife – Katherine Blount – predeceased him in 1559 (1560?), whereas the second, Elizabeth Sands, survived until 1585.

Sir Maurice was a powerful and influential figure, having been standard-bearer to a succession of Tudor monarchs, including Henry VIII, Edward VI and Elizabeth I. He also, however, proved loyal to Queen Mary during Wyatt's Rebellion in 1554, and accepted the surrender of Sir Thomas Wyatt himself. Berkeley's ascending star saw him join the household of Thomas Cromwell in 1537 or 1538 on his way to joining the royal household a year or so later. Given his political prominence, a great deal of his time would have been spent at Court, but he had a mansion built on the site of Bruton Priory which was itself demolished in turn in 1786.

Elsewhere in the church may be found a rather battered fifteenth-century chest tomb, and a notable wall monument which commemorates the short life of William Godolphin (1611-1636) who was Governor of the Scilly Isles. This duty cannot have been an overly onerous one, for he assumed the position in 1613 at the age of two. The church also possesses some fine Jacobean woodcarving in the form of a chancel screen dating from 1620, which was moved some time ago to its present position beneath the tower arch. If you should find yourself in Bruton, St Mary's is certainly worth a visit. You'll likely find much more of interest than noted here.

Witchcraft in Castle Cary

There are doubtless folk in this market town who would today describe themselves as 'witches', but in 1530, before the witch mania had reached its peak, a certain Isabel Turner found herself charged with witchcraft by several of her fellow townsfolk. The nature of the charges reveals their rootedness in pronounced personal enmity and mistrust, which often proved to be the case with such allegations. Christian Shirston, after being denied a quart of ale by Turner, stated that at that very instant 'a stand of ale of twelve gallons began to boil as fast as a crock on the fire.' Joan Vicars's cow ceased yielding milk, offering up blood and water instead, after she refused Turner milk. Henry Russe, who also refused her milk, was then unable to make cheese. What became of Isabel Turner? I could not discover.

Tomb of Sir Maurice Berkeley and Wives

Tomb of Sir Maurice Berkeley and Wives

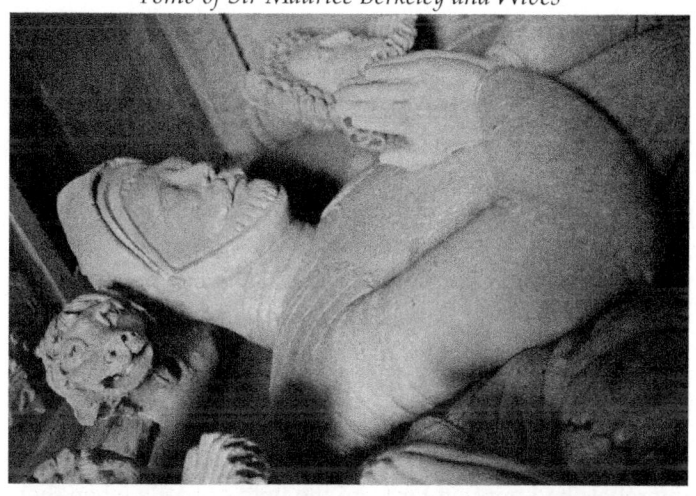

Cothelstone

Cothelstone's Hanging Gateway

The triple-arched stone gateway, which now bestrides the entrance to the driveway of Cothelstone Manor in Somerset, once stood across the neighbouring road. When it was moved to its present position to ease the passage of traffic is unclear, although it is mentioned that this occurred at some point before 1908, so presumably a picture of the gateway shows it as being here in that year. Whereas the structure possesses a certain charm, its stones were once put to rather gruesome usage in the year 1685 in the wake of the ill-fated Sedgemoor Rebellion. As the old milestone next to the gate indicates, it is only some nine miles to Bridgwater (here spelt in the more logical old-fashioned way as Bridgewater), so the rebels had not fled far from the field of battle when they were hunted down by the forces of retribution that swiftly followed upon the heels of their defeat. And so it was that two members of Monmouth's army came to be hanged from its arches: Thomas Blackmore, and Colonel Richard Bovett of Monmouth's Blue Regiment.

It is said that the gateway was chosen by Judge Jeffreys as a place of execution and display out of a fit of pique, for although Ralph Stawell had remained loyal to the Crown during the rising, he was repelled by the unforgiving and bloody retribution meted out by Jeffreys in its wake. It was this sense of disgust that led him to deny Jeffreys a bed at his home, and so the judge decreed that his gateway should be adorned with corpses. How long they were left hanging there is not mentioned, nor what became of their bodies afterwards.

The Gateway to Cothelstone Manor

Cothelstone Manor and Holy Well

The manor itself is set back from the road, obscuring the parish church to its rear where the lords and ladies of Cothelstone were ultimately laid to rest. At the edge of a field close to the manor is a charming stone-walled structure with a corbelled roof named St Agnes Holy Well. Dating back to the late-mediaeval period, a certain amount of folklore has come to be attached to it over the centuries. The locals, it would seem, once regarded it with a sense of wary fascination, for on the one hand it was said that if a virgin were to visit the well on the Eve of St Agnes – 20 January – then the identity of her future husband would be revealed, but on the other it was claimed to be the haunt of mischievous pixies, and thus best avoided. Indeed, a nearby stream is named the 'Pixie Stream'.

Returning to the manor, its origins are believed to lie in the Saxon period. A legend claims that it was the Saxon leader, Cuthwulf (c. 592-648), sent to the borders of

Dumnonia in around 620, who here founded a religious retreat with his wife, a Dumnonian princess named Gwynhafar. He raised it in fulfilment of a vow upon returning from a reputed pilgrimage to the Holy Land. The discovery of ancient foundations in its grounds during the nineteenth century seemed to lend some credence to this myth. From 1087, and possibly a little earlier, until the end of the eighteenth century, the manor remained in the hands of a single family: the Covestons, who later took the name of Stawell. Both the main house and gatehouse that we see today were built in the middle of the sixteenth century, but such a pummelling did the manor take from the cannon of parliamentarian forces under Colonel (later 'Admiral') Blake in 1646, that much of its structure was demolished. It would not be until the mid-1850s that it was rebuilt by the Esdaile family in its present form. It is, so far as I am aware, currently privately let, and not therefore open to the public.

Cothelstone Manor from the Neighbouring Churchyard

Monuments and Curiosities of Cothelstone's Parish Church
Behind the manor stands the Church of St Thomas of Canterbury, an attractive stone-built structure dating from the fifteenth century, with earlier elements from the twelfth and thirteenth, its red sandstone exuding warmth. Those with a taste for monumental tombs and vernacular woodcarving will not be disappointed, for here may be seen memorials to the Stawell family, as well as a number of characterful carved bench ends. Two of the tombs are surmounted by pairs of effigies, the earlier of them raised in honour of Sir Matthew de Stawell (died 1379) and his wife Eleanor. He is, as typical for the period, shown in full armour, and sporting a magnificent moustache. His wife, on the other hand, is neither armoured nor moustached, a fact which I should imagine must have pleased him. A gap of more than two centuries separates this tomb from the second and rather more impressive memorial to Sir John Stawell (1536-1603), and his wife Frances. Their effigies, beautifully carved in alabaster, have survived relatively unscathed despite the tomb having been moved during a thoroughgoing restoration of the church in the nineteenth century, a repositioning which resulted in the loss of its original canopy. It was their son, also named Sir John, who would see his estates expropriated and sold off for the then vast sum of £64,000 in 1651, having fought for the losing Royalist cause. He would, however, live to see his fortunes wax once more, for with the Restoration came the return of his estates which he was to enjoy for but a brief period, as he died on 21 February 1662 (1661 old style, reckoning the year as starting on Lady Day – 25th March). His memorial is situated on the wall of the chancel opposite a brief inscription commemorating the life of his father.

For those who have come to explore the Quantocks and their associations with the Romantic poets, it is perhaps worth mentioning that in the churchyard lies the grave of Iolanthe Esdaile, the daughter of Percy Bysshe Shelley.

Crowcombe's Church of the Holy Ghost, and a Haunting
It is thought that a place of worship stood here in Saxon times, although no documentary evidence makes mention of it by name until 1226. A quintessential English parish church, with its tower dating from the fourteenth century and the rest of the structure predominantly from the fifteenth, the Church of the Holy Ghost in the village of Crowcombe can surely look no more appealing to the eye than when mantled with snow and set against a blue sky. Its red sandstone adds warm notes to so chilly a scene, but it once, at least for a brief moment, glowed rather hotter, for in December 1724 its spire was struck by lightning. No small damage was done, and the spire never rebuilt. Indeed, the uppermost portion of the latter now lies planted towards the eastern wall of the churchyard, looking far less impressive than the fourteenth-century preaching cross that stands close to the church porch. Other fragments of the spire were subsequently incorporated into the church floor.

The octagonal font is a pretty affair, carved from yellow sandstone and dating from the late fourteenth or early fifteenth century, and would likely draw the eye of the visitor more readily if it were not for the diverting sight of the truly wondrous collection of carved bench ends that are now approaching the five-hundredth anniversary of their carving. Likewise, look above when you enter the church porch and you will see a fine example of fan vaulting, intricately carved from the same sandstone.

Sitting upon a rise overlooking the main village street, the church, like Crowcombe itself, is now largely undisturbed. Its tranquillity is thanks to the efforts of a certain Mrs Trollope, an erstwhile Lady of the Manor who successfully campaigned for a bypass to be built. She had taken umbrage at the noise and disruption occasioned by the passage of heavy lorries on their way to and from the local quarries. This simply would not do, and so she went so far as to donate some of her own land for the building of a new road. However, its construction necessitated the demolition of an outlying cottage, a humble dwelling which happened to be inhabited by an old woman who possessed quite an attachment to the place, but move she had to and move she did. She was re-housed as compensation, but her new home could not replace her old, and so shortly afterwards she pined away, and died. Since that time, there have been reports of sightings of a strange and lonely figure wandering the bypass, a bunch of flowers clutched in her hands: the forlorn and heartbroken ghost of the old lady. Of her home, nothing more remains than a tangled patch of brambles at the edge of the tarmac highway, where once her cottage garden bloomed.

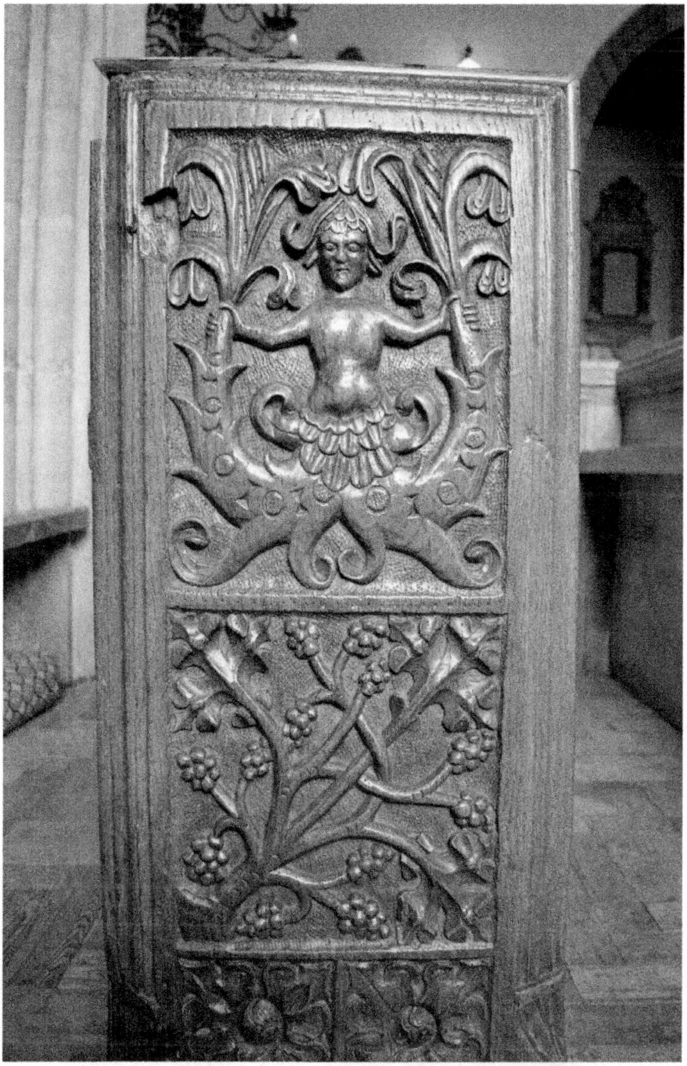

162

Can you decipher the date?

Fanciful Carvings on the Bench Ends of Crowcombe Church

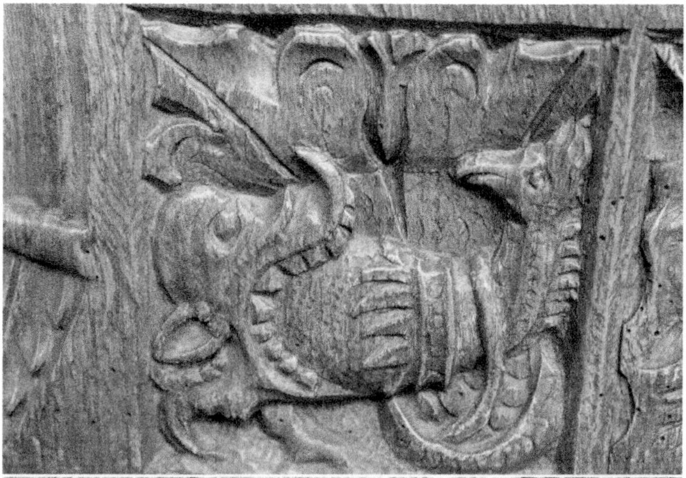

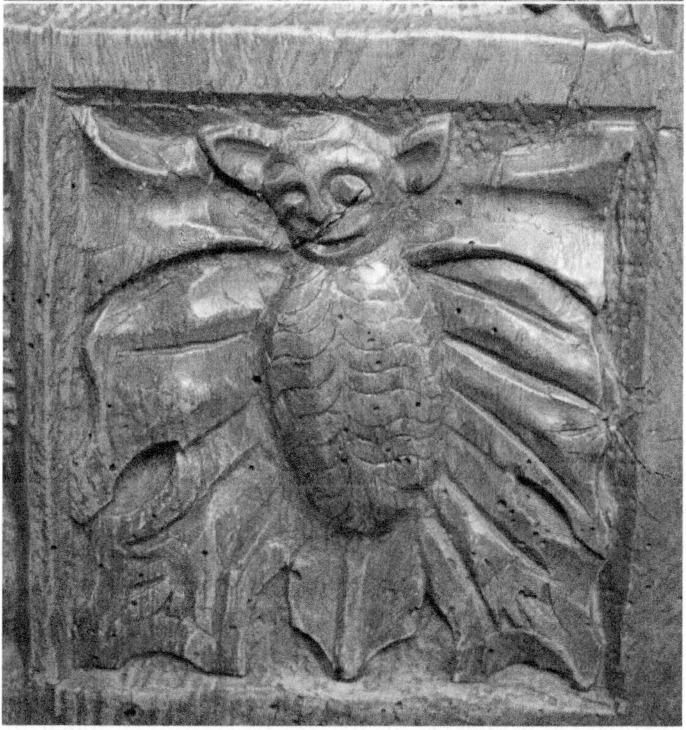

Crowcombe's Wild Hunt

It would seem that the village also boasts, or once boasted, a tale which was its own variation upon the theme of the Wild Hunt. Noted down by folklorist Ruth Tongue in 1935, it was narrated by a local woman who stated that local tradition held that a huntsman would frequent the area, his quarry taking the form of a white hare, which was held to embody the soul of an unredeemed sinner. He himself was of quite singular appearance, possessed of a pair of poorly-concealed modest horns that protruded from beneath his cap, and a single cloven hoof. Each of his hounds also sported horns, yet his horse had no head at all. In the heat of the baying chase his hounds would swish and whip their tails in a burning sulphurous cloud through which glowered their reddened and fiery eyes.

The Haunting of Dead Woman's Ditch

High up on the Quantock Hills between the villages of Crowcombe and Over Stowey is a local beauty spot named Dead Woman's Ditch. Although reputedly named after the vicious murder of Jane Walford here by her husband in 1789, it is, apparently, shown as bearing this same name on earlier maps. So, perhaps, some other ghastly crime happened to precede it.

Over the years there have been reports of ghostly goings-on in and around Dead Woman's Ditch. Generally, they concern the sighting of a female figure all in white and dressed in 'old-fashioned clothing', which is sometimes described as 'bright' in appearance, suggesting that she may possess something of a glow. However, despite the icy serenity conjured by such a vision, her temper would appear to be rather hot, for the last couple to report encountering her state that the spirit yelled at them to 'Fuck off!' Such an utterance, it would seem, may have been very much in keeping with Jane Walford's character, if the sad story connected with the circumstances of her death is anything to go by. After all, John Walford was by all accounts a popular fellow, known by both Wordsworth and Coleridge when they lived in the district.

John was a hard-working charcoal burner, possessed of both good looks and temper alike, who one day fell in love with a local woman by the name of Ann Rice. There was an understanding that the two would marry, but somehow John fell for the dubious charms of Jane Shorney, whose appearance, if contemporary accounts are anything to believe, were less than prepossessing, she being described as 'stupid', 'squat' and 'disgustingly dirty and slovenly'. Sadly for the both of them, he got her pregnant. The child was born into bastardy, and so John's engagement to Ann fell through. Having made Jane pregnant a second time, he had no other option than to marry her. Their marriage was miserable from the outset, and before a fortnight was out he confided with a friend that he wished to abscond to London. Apparently, Ann Rice too was carrying his child. Jane repeatedly taunted him regarding his love for Ann with a spiteful relish. He snapped. Just three weeks after their marriage when the two of them were returning from the Castle of Comfort Inn, Jane instigated yet another argument. It was past midnight, and in a moment of drunken rage he grabbed her by the throat, beat her unconscious, and finally slit her throat. The flow of words was replaced by the slick flow of blood.

Jane's body was soon discovered, and John immediately confessed to the crime. He was sentenced to death by hanging, and duly driven by cart to Danesborough Hill where a gallows had been erected. Ann wished him a final farewell, and once his body had finished with its twitching and kicking it was taken down and encased in an iron cage.

Raised to the top of the gibbet, it remained on prominent display, clearly visible from his parents' front door, for a year and a day until it was taken down. It is rumoured that his spirit is as restless as his wife's, for there have been reports of hearing his ghostly footsteps in the vicinity of where the gibbet once stood.

A Strange Tale from Dunster

A friend of mine recently spent a few days in the picturesque village of Dunster, which, as many of you know, lies on the edge of Exmoor. It is a bustling little place, its main street mobbed by tourists, many of whom have come to visit its castle from where fine views of this westernmost corner of the county may be enjoyed. And it is a place that possesses its own fair share of folklore, especially when it comes to ghosts and hauntings. However, the story I am about to relate concerns nothing that may be said to be spectral in nature, although it may be adjudged to be equally unorthodox. This is what my friend told me.

Early one evening, having left his wife to her own devices in the village, he'd headed off for a solo walk on the wooded slopes of one of the neighbouring hills. It had been a warm day, and the light was still good. All was as tranquil and pleasing as he could have hoped it to be, as the dappled sunlight played upon the woodland floor, and he wandered alone with his thoughts. For quite how long he walked in his own company he cannot recall, for when immersed in such solitary pleasure's one's sense of time is apt to drift. But that he was alone, and had been alone, he did not for one moment doubt. And then, he was made rudely aware of the fact that he was not. There was a loud crack, as of a piece of rotten wood snapping underfoot. His head whipped round as more sounds issued from the undergrowth, betraying the presence of some person, or animal, unseen. And then, for but the most fleeting of moments, he caught sight of it. His view, alas, was unclear, for its body was partially obscured by trees and vegetation, but his impression was that its form was long and held relatively low to the ground, with its most striking feature being its 'pointed ears. Black pointed ears of the velvety blackness of moleskin.'

To say that his heart missed a beat or two would be something of an understatement, but then the succession of sounds came to a sudden stop. Their cessation, however, brought not a sense of relief, but of alarm. The creature had paused, although of it he could see nothing more than that pair of black pointed ears, from the sight of which he divined the animal held him within its none-too-friendly regard. And then, in an instant, it was gone.

Putting aside his apprehensions, his sense of curiosity led him from the path, and he set off in pursuit. A little while later he happened upon a depression, and approaching it with caution, realised that something sat within. Was this then the creature's lair? The thought gave him pause, so he crept forward cautiously, hoping neither to alert nor startle it. Silence. Whatever it was, it did not move. Something bulky now lay before him below, but as he drew closer, expecting to behold a pair of black pointed ears attached to a low-slung body, he saw instead . . . a large log. Thereupon he decided to walk back to the village, and nothing more unusual did he see that evening other than whatever dreams were prompted by a few pints of Exmoor Gold. Had he glimpsed the fabled Beast of Exmoor?

The Artistic Highlights of St Mary's Church, East Brent
Nothing in the fabric of the present church is thought to predate the thirteenth century, although the manor of Brent

was presented to the monks of Glastonbury Abbey in 693 and remained the property of that foundation until its dissolution in 1539. Still, there is much of interest here to attract the attention of the visitor. Its west tower and spire make for an imposing sight, and whereas the niches of many such towers have long since been emptied of their original works of sculpture, here three pieces of note may be viewed: one representing Christ crowning the Blessed Virgin; a second depicting the Holy Trinity; and a third the Virgin and Child, rather unusually sitting upon a corbel decorated with a human face from which foliage liberally spews: a green man. Although these sculptures have borne the brunt of centuries of weathering, they are still clear enough as to be readily recognisable. Elsewhere in the churchyard may be seen a mysterious recumbent effigy attired in what would appear to be fifteenth, or possibly early sixteenth, century costume. His head resting on a pillow, he sports a gown with voluminous sleeves which hang down from his hands clasped in prayer, whilst billowing pleated skirts cover his legs to just below the knees. Might he have been a merchant?

Inside St Mary's are two other effigies which lie recessed in the church walls. Both are thought to be priests, although their identities, as well as their ages, are uncertain. One, it is speculated, dates from the fourteenth century, although in the same breath the church guide mentions that this very same piece of sculpture may represent Martin de Summa who lived in the twelfth century. The better preserved of the pair sports a fringe befitting of Slade guitarist Dave Hill.

The church also boasts a fine collection of carved bench ends thought to date from the fifteenth century, one featuring the familiar motif of the pelican plucking at her breast to feed blood to her young. As with virtually all mediaeval depictions of this bird, it bears scant resemblance to an actual pelican. A later piece which amply demonstrates the talents of the woodcarver is the intricately adorned oak pulpit which dates from 1634. There is also a particularly well preserved example of late-mediaeval stained glass in the sixth window of the North Aisle depicting three figures, including St James with his hat emblazoned with his emblematic scallop shell. It is a truly beautiful piece of work. Other stained glass from this period has not faired quite so well, and a jumble of mediaeval fragments may be seen set in two other windows.

Mediaeval Stained Glass, St Mary's Church, East Brent

Carved Bench End, St Mary's Church, East Brent

The Church of St Edward the Martyr, Goathurst

Although only a handful of miles from the town of Bridgwater, the village of Goathurst (pronounced Go Thirst rather than Goat Hurst) appears an isolated place. Accessed via a tangle of narrow winding lanes, it is somewhere best left to itself when the tarmac is sheened with black ice, as I'd recommend from personal experience. Still, the trip, which was something of an afterthought, proved worthwhile, and all mishaps were avoided. What had drawn me here was a rather interesting tomb that I had only a few days earlier stumbled across online, and it didn't disappoint.

The monument in question was raised in honour of Sir Nicholas and Lady Bridgett Halswell. Situated in the Halswell family chapel of Goathurst's parish church of St Edward the Martyr, it looks quite splendid in a morbid sort of way, and if the number of 'weepers' at the base of the tomb is anything to go by, their marriage was a fruitful one: six sons and three daughters, each dutifully depicted in prayerful aspect. Side by side the couple lies, hands clasped in prayer, eyes wide open staring blankly at the arcaded canopy as if reposing in some grand tester bed attired in their magnificent ruffed Jacobean finery, Sir Nicholas in his armour, and Lady Bridgett in flowing dress and shroud. She was the first to die, on 28 July 1627, whereas he survived her by almost six years, dying on 1 May 1633. But what of their lives? What do we know of them?

Sir Nicholas was baptised on the last day of November 1566, and as a young man went on to study at Magdalen College, Oxford, before marrying Bridgett, whose family – the Wallops – hailed from Fairleigh Wallop in Hampshire. Knighted in 1603, he held a number of positions befitting a gentleman of his station. Between 1596 and 1626 he acted as a Justice of the Peace, and it was whilst fulfilling this office that in 1608 he was called upon to deal with a minister of a somewhat fanatical and unorthodox bent from the neighbouring village of North Petherton: John Gilbert, also known as John Gogulmere. The people of that parish called upon Sir Nicholas to act when the said Gilbert made an attempt one 'Sabbath day' to preach to his congregation within the walls of St Mary's dressed in nothing more than Adam before his adoption of a fig leaf. This early experiment in naturism led to the imprisonment of its enthusiastic exponent, but what then became of him I do not know.

Sir Nicholas also held responsibilities at various times connected to the maintenance of sewers, hospitals, almshouses, and the court of oyer and terminer, and from 1604 to 1614 served as MP for Bridgwater, before effectively passing on this office to his eldest son, Robert. Parliamentary records would suggest that he was not the most voluble of members, for only one known speech is recorded, in which he volunteered to explain the absence of his brother-in-law – Sir Richard Paulet – from the Commons. This apparent silence, however, should not indicate that he was an inactive MP, for he was involved in the work of a number of parliamentary committees. Later in life he was to suffer serious financial difficulties on account of lending considerable sums of money to prominent Somerset individuals who would subsequently default on their loans.

When he died intestate in 1633, his estate passed for a brief period to his son Henry. Upon the latter's death it became the property of his younger brother, Dr Hugh Halswell, a clergymen who died without male heirs in 1672. During the Second World War Halswell House hosted a relocated girls' school, as well as an Italian prisoner-of-war camp. By the end of the war it had become a shabby semblance of its former self, was broken up into lots and auctioned off. In 2009, the Palladian Halswell House, which stands close to its Tudor predecessor, was let out to a Dutch company for a masked ball. What the then owner did not anticipate was that upon the stroke of midnight the 350 revellers would whip off their clothing and indulge in a mass orgy. What the long-dead Sir Nicholas, who tried and sentenced a naked canting preacher, have made of that?

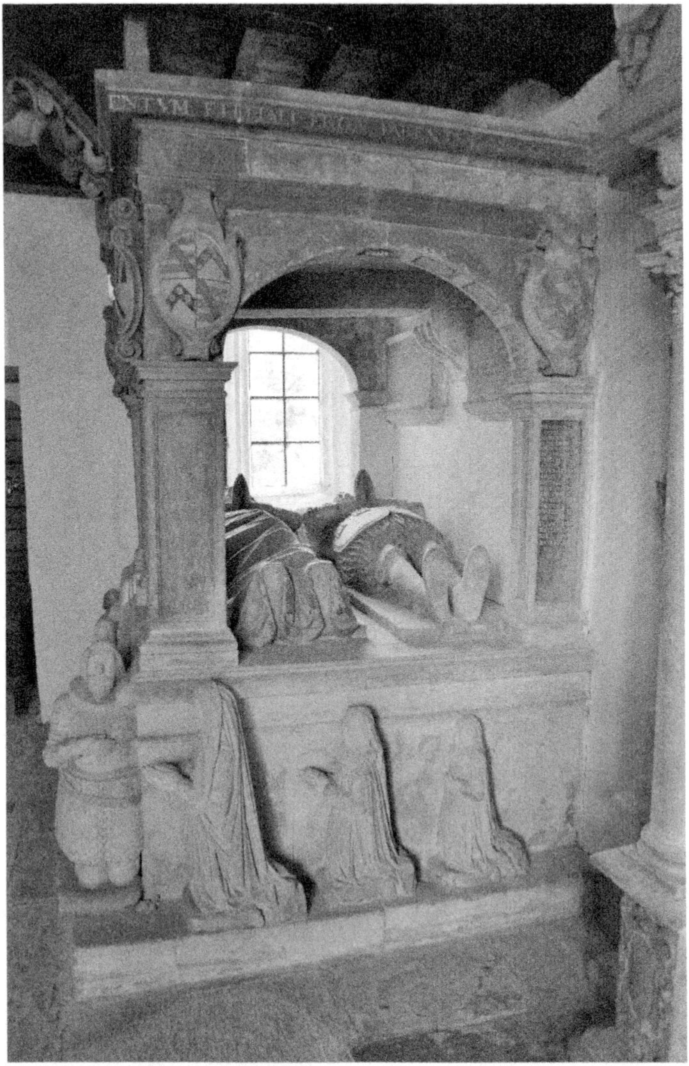

The church boasts two other memorials worthy of attention. One is a striking and rather poignant effigy of the slumbering Isabella Anne Kemeys, who died at the age of three. She was, however, buried not here at Goathurst, but far away in the Cooper family vault in Chilton Foliat, Wiltshire. The second is an elaborate Palladian wall memorial to the immediate descendants of Sir Nicholas and Lady Bridgett Halswell. Its lengthy text is carved in Latin, with the monument itself being surmounted by cherubs and memento mori.

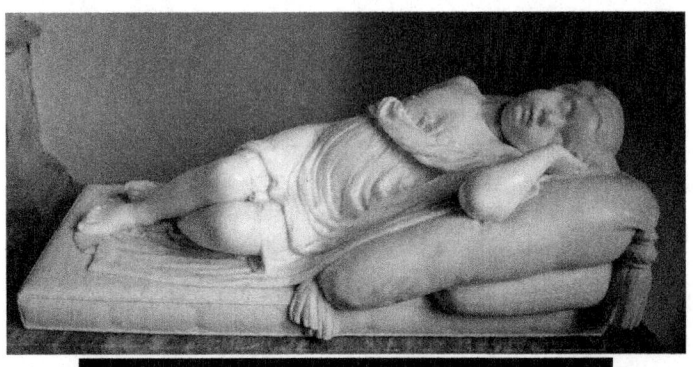

Fifteenth-Century Font, Goathurst

Blue Ben of Kilve

Just along the Severn coast from Watchet is the village of Kilve. It is a small place that according to local legend once boasted a rather large resident: Blue Ben, a fiery dragon which dwelt in neighbouring Putsham Hill. He was not, it would seem, a particularly happy creature, for he disliked being dreadfully hot, and would therefore frequently repair to the shore to take a cooling dip in the waters of the Bristol Channel. There was, however, a problem: before he could reach the water he had to negotiate a series of mudflats, and not wishing to become mired in them he built a causeway of rocks so that he might make his way to and from his favoured bathing spot without covering himself in mud.

Looking towards Kilve from Watchet

The Devil got to hear of Blue Ben, and thinking him an ideal mount to charge about his hellish realm took the beast from his lair beneath the hill and put him into harness. Having worked the dragon hard and made him hotter still, Ben somehow managed to escape and rushed up to the surface.

So anxious was the dragon to cool itself that it rushed with such haste that it lost its balance upon the causeway, and slipping fell promptly into the mud which claimed him. And the evidence, so the story goes, is there for all to see, for some locals aver that the fossilised skull of an ichthyosaurus quarried from the shale near Kilve early in the nineteenth century belongs to none other than Blue Ben.

Nether Stowey Castle: its History, and Folklore
Silently brooding above the Somerset village of Nether Stowey, is a large earthen mound surrounded by a pronounced ditch. This is the motte of its motte and bailey, or, more accurately, motte and two bailey castle. Long since abandoned, the site is now given over to rough pasture, its stone having been robbed out and used in the construction of a number of pleasing dwellings in the village below. Of its great hall, which once stood in one of its baileys, nothing remains to be seen, although if you climb the motte itself you will find, still visible and set into its top, the sturdy footings of the castle keep. That is all. The grandeur that may once have been, is no more.

Whether the castle, raised in the late eleventh or early twelfth centuries, and abandoned from the end of the fifteenth, inspired fear, respect or affection, I shall leave to your imagination. But, there is one piece of folklore attached to this place that is suggestive of the opinion that once prevailed hereabouts. Whimsical it may be, but it is no less telling for that: it concerns the 'Giants of Stowey'. The story runs as follows.

Long ago a group of giants threw up the mound of Stowey Castle, dwelling like massive moles beneath it. There was consternation amongst the locals. Those who were able-bodied fled to neighbouring Stogursey, or to the relative safety of the ramparts of the hillfort of Dowsborough Camp. Only the infirm and the very young remained.

The giants, as you might have guessed, possessed appetites equal to their stature, and thus were apt to grab at passing sheep, cows, and occasionally people. They troughed the lot. Folk were thus not a little nervous about venturing within reach of the grasping arms that flailed out from the castle; the spot was shunned. But once the giants had tasted human flesh, they came to esteem it above all other, and having exhausted the supply of unwitting passers-by, tumbled out of their mound in search of a delicacy which they had come to desire as their staple. Strangely, rather than raiding the village on their doorstep, they took themselves off to Stogursey and there beat down the walls of its castle, grabbing up and scoffing locals by the handful until there were few if any left. Then, and only then, did they return their ogreish attentions to Nether Stowey.

The flesh of the youngsters they found soft enough, albeit perhaps a little bland, whereas that of the elderly made for tough chewing. Still, eat they must, so the giants persevered. One old chap attempted to steal past the castle in search of help from the folk hiding out at Dowsborough, but the hands had him, and into the pot he went. It was left to a little lad to save the day. Mounting one of his father's ponies, he set off at a fair gallop in the direction of Dowsborough. All about him galloped every pony that belonged to his family, shielding him from the grasping hands. Hearing the commotion down below, the men of the camp took up arms, and welcoming the boy surged out to do battle with the giants of Stowey. They beat them good and proper, smashing down the walls of the castle, and setting the giants affright. The folk of Nether Stowey have never been troubled by them since, although it's said that there's still a certain reluctance to pass the castle mound at night.

Coleridge in Somerset

From 1797 to 1799, the Romantic poet Samuel Taylor Coleridge rented a cottage in the village of Nether Stowey. Despite thinking it a mouse-infested 'hovel', whilst there he was moved to compose a number of his most famous works, including *The Rime of the Ancient Mariner* and *Kubla Khan*, as well as making a start upon both *Christabel* and *Frost at Midnight*.

For over a century, Coleridge Cottage, as it has come to be known, has been in the hands of the National Trust and is open to the public. Much of it has been furnished and decorated to appear as it would have done during the period of Coleridge's residence here with his young wife Sara, and contains a number of artefacts and pieces of memorabilia associated with the poet.

Coleridge Cottage, Nether Stowey

Whilst living in Nether Stowey, William Wordsworth and his sister Dorothy rented nearby Alfoxton Park, an altogether grander affair, from July 1797 to the June of the following year, and the two poets were in regular contact. They had first become acquainted in 1795, and would jointly publish the volume *Lyrical Ballads* in 1798. The Wordsworths were the first to leave Somerset for the Lake District town of Keswick, followed by the Coleridges in December 1799, but there was to be no happy ending. Coleridge came to abhor his wife, and the couple finally separated in 1808, their marriage having produced four children.

Returning to Somerset, it was the harbour at Watchet which provided inspiration for the port in *The Rime of the Ancient Mariner*. The Bell Inn, close to the waterfront, was where Coleridge wrote the first lines of the poem, and in 2003 the town's harbour was graced with a striking statue of the Ancient Mariner, albatross tied about his neck, created by sculptor Alan B. Herriot. As for *Kubla Khan*, it would take almost twenty years for it to appear in print on account of it not having been completed; it never would be, all down to Coleridge having been interrupted during its composition by a 'person from Porlock', or so he claimed. After an hour drawn away from his opium-induced literary vision, or 'dream' as he termed it, he averred that he was not then able to recall what was to take place after the initial fifty-four lines that he had composed. Once the initial inspiration had departed . . . well. Coleridge's opium habit would not serve him well, with the side effects of constipation and physical dependency vastly outweighing any temporary creative stimulus that he may have derived from the drug. Indeed, by 1814 he had come to acknowledge laudanum as a 'free-agency-annihilating poison.'

The Ancient Mariner, Watchet Harbour

The Galley-Beggar of Over Stowey

Quite where the 'galley-beggar' gets its name from I've no idea, although it is reputed, according to former folklorist Ruth Tongue, to have been the moniker of a particular hobgoblin that once frequented (or, indeed, still frequents for all that I know) the slopes between Over Stowey and Nether Stowey. It is a simple and merry soul, whose head sits not in its usual place, but is carried beneath its arm as it toboggans on a wooden hurdle down the hillside in the dead of night, shrieking and laughing with an uncontainable delight.

An article entitled *Tradition and Folklore of the Quantocks* published in 1907 by the Rev. Chas. Whistler forwards an interesting speculation as to its origins, although he simply refers to it as a 'ghost' rather than by this singular name. In his opinion, it likely originates as a folk memory related to the execution of one of the followers of Lord Audley of Stowey who supported Perkin Warbeck in his abortive rebellion against Henry VII in 1497. After all, Warbeck himself was drawn to the scaffold on a hurdle, then beheaded.

There is another tradition of a headless supernatural entity said to have frequented one of the deep hillside lanes of the Quantocks, this time a ghost that carried his head beneath his arm. The Rev. Whistler was moved to speculate that it was likely 'a relic from Saxon days', for he notes that it was the custom in those distant times to disinter and decapitate a corpse that had proven restless in its grave, before reburying it with its head placed alongside its body. If so, such a precaution in this instance would seem to have been singularly ineffective.

Nether Stowey Castle

Nether Stowey Castle

Priddy

Sitting on top of the Mendip plateau, the village of Priddy is surrounded by reminders of the distant past. Whereas a Mesolithic hut site was excavated here in 1977, it is the Neolithic that bestows the first visual evidence of human settlement in the area. Nearby North Hill hosts two groups of barrows – Priddy Nine Barrows and Ashen Hill – whilst just to the north of the hill are four Neolithic earthwork enclosures, presumed to be henge-type monuments. Named the Priddy Circles, their function is obscure, hence their characterisation by archaeologists as 'ritual'. The origins of Priddy's name have also occasioned lively speculation, with the majority of suggested derivations linking it to Brythonic.

Areas of 'gruffy ground' close to the village are associated with lead mining, which is believed to have commenced in the area some two to three centuries before the Roman Conquest. Indeed, the lure of lead is thought to have been one of the motivating factors for the Claudian invasion, and a small Roman town grew up at nearby Charterhouse where both lead and silver were mined. Its traces may still be divined in the landscape today, most notably in the form of a small amphitheatre, as well as in the hummocky ground left by the mines themselves. A legend also grew up that Joseph of Arimathea had brought Jesus to Priddy on one of his trading voyages to Britain in search of lead.

Beneath Priddy run the passages of Swildon's Hole, the longest cave system in the Mendip Hills, home to magnificent chambers and treacherous sumps; a secret subterranean world that first revealed itself to the human eye in 1901.

Turning, finally, to the recorded history of the village, it was for several centuries perhaps best known for its annual sheep fair. Its origins lay in one of the greatest calamities to ever hit England – the Black Death – for the fair was moved to Priddy from Wells in 1348 to escape the worst ravages of the pestilence. Almost every year thereafter the fair would be held here, an occasion for celebration as well as for the buying and selling of sheep. A longstanding symbol of this event was a stack of hurdles which stood on the village green, topped with a thatched roof. Over the centuries, those which decayed and broke were replaced in a piecemeal way. There grew up a legend that if the hurdles were ever removed, then the fair itself would end. On 28 April 2013, an arsonist set light to the stack, destroying it completely. The police identified a suspect, but were unable to prosecute owing to insufficient evidence. The 2014 fair was cancelled owing to health and safety considerations, and it has never run since. However, as can be seen from the picture below, a new hurdle stack was made and sits on the green today. Although the fair has now been consigned to the past, there is a new fixture in the annual round: the Priddy Folk Festival.

Heathen Echoes in the Folklore of the Quantocks

There is a trackway of great antiquity that led from the village of Combwich on the River Parrett to Dowsborough Camp – a hillfort whose origins lie in the Iron Age – on the Quantocks. Named the Herepath, it functioned as a military road during the reign of King Alfred, with a spur named the Great Bear Path (Great Herepath) providing the link to Dowsborough. It connected a number of lookouts and strongpoints raised to watch for raiders in the Bristol Channel, although according to folklore still current in the nineteenth century it also provided a route for something besides mere mortal traffic. These otherworldly travellers included a headless lone rider upon a black steed; a horseman chasing a fierce pack of flaming-eyed black dogs, with his mount this time being headless; and a massive pig ridden through the air chasing after the same diabolical pack of hounds. The Rev. Whistler equated these three riders with memories of the Norse gods Odin, Thor, and Frey respectively, with the massive hog being none other than the boar Gullinbursti ('Golden Bristles').

Along this same track we encounter another folktale with echoes of pre-Christian heathenry. As it is associated with a location below Dowsborough named Wayland's Pond, or Wayland's Pool, and involves a smith of exceptional talent, we may take it that its origins, perhaps, are connected to the figure of Wayland the Smith. It is said that he used the said pool to cool and temper his horseshoes. The story goes that his smithy was situated in Keenthorne at a junction with the Herepath, and so proud was he of his skill that he bragged he might shoe even the Devil's own horse if he should so happen to call. Little did he expect that he might have the opportunity of making good so idle a boast. It was midnight when he was called down from his bed by a traveller whose horse had cast its shoe. Letting the stranger lead his handsome black mount into the smithy, he could not help but notice that the rider himself too was possessed of a hoof. In a supreme effort of will, he managed to conceal his sense of horror from his visitor, and pleading the excuse that he had to fetch his shoeing hammer from the village, made straight to the vicarage. He arrived in some distress and begged the parson for assistance, but the latter offered nothing more than the advice that on no account should he accept payment for his work, for if he did so then the Devil would surely claim his soul.

Disappointed and his mind still ill at ease, the smith returned to undertake the work that he had agreed. The parson, meanwhile, followed and hid himself behind a hedge so that he might watch proceedings unobserved. As promised, the horse was shod and shod well, with the Devil being so mightily pleased that he lavished praise upon the smith, and offered to reward him handsomely, but the smith was quite insistent that he would accept no payment. Suspicious as to the cause of the smith's refusal, the Devil looked about him, and espied the cowering parson. With a vexatious exclamation, both the rider and his horse instantly 'vanished in a flash of fire.'

Wayland also possesses associations with the Wild Hunt, and it would therefore seem appropriate that this story should be connected to the route taken by the trio of otherworldly huntsmen mentioned above. Many years after the events of this tale were said to have taken place, the junction was still regarded with a degree of unease by local waggoners and coachmen, whose horses reputedly displayed erratic behaviour at that particular spot. Something was spooking them. Its ill reputation was cemented still further by it having lain close to the abode of a local witch. Indeed, witchcraft lingered long in the district, employed for good as well as for ill, with the following cure for warts having once been used: first, make a broth from slow worms, and having done so anoint the affected hand whilst invoking the Holy Trinity. As to the precise verbal formula to be employed, that has been lost.

Wayland the Smith (left) depicted on the Franks Casket

Snowy Scene on the Quantocks

St Decuman's Church, Watchet: She Only Lived Twice

But a year into her marriage and heavy with child, tragedy was to strike: Florence Wyndham, in the tender bloom of her womanhood, was declared dead at the age of twenty. This was, after all, 1558, and a youthful death was far from uncommon, even for a wealthy heiress lately married into the Somerset nobility. Whether her husband, Sir John, stood in Watchet's parish Church of St Decuman's stoical and dry-eyed, or wept in profusion as the priest read her eulogy, we can only guess, although we are told that his grief was great. And as the pomp and ceremony of the funeral service drew to a close, her coffin was taken down into the Wyndham vault, and there it was laid.

The mourners filed away, and that night but one man found himself alone in the church, whom tradition has unreliably recorded as being either the sexton, or the verger. And the tale, so it seems, may have gained much in the telling, so it is up to you whether you should choose to look upon this fellow with a charitable or a jaundiced eye. He had come, some say, spurred by the spirit of greed, and so it was that he was moved to enter the vault and prise open the lid of the coffin. There before his eyes glinted the rings on her fingers. Did he then hesitate before he took his file to the first ring? Had he ever undertaken such a ghoulish venture before? Such details are left unsaid. But he did not, at least according to one version of the story, employ rough butchery in the attempted removal of that precious band of metal from its rightful place, for he sought not to slice off any of her fingers. Yet his work with his file was not so delicate that he did not cut the flesh and draw blood. At this point, Lady Wyndham awoke, and with a groan and fixing the terrified sexton with opened eyes, announced her return to the living. The man fled, never to show his face again in the parish, whereas she, awakened from her catalepsy, rose from her coffin, and upon unsteady feet staggered through and out of the church, homeward bound.

It was the servants who opened the door to her knock, and beholding her figure in its grave clothes took her for some supernatural vision, but whether she were a ghost or a witch they knew not. Upon beholding the semblance of his wife, Sir John fell into a faint, and was taken off to his bed. Such evil could not be admitted to the house, and so she remained at the door the night long, locked out of her own home. And when the door was opened the following morning, there they found Lady Florence in the throes of labour. She gave birth to a son, who would be named John after his father. And all of the subsequent Wyndhams hailed their descent from this child, a boy born of a woman who had lain in the coldness of the crypt. Lady Florence would outlive her husband by a good many years, passing away in 1596. Her likeness may be seen in St Decuman's today, etched in brass opposite her beloved Sir John.

The oldest part of St Decuman's is its chancel, dating back to the late twelfth century. Its floor is decorated with a number of beautiful thirteenth-century floor tiles, believed to have possibly been brought here from nearby Cleeve Abbey. Lines of wooden angels may be seen flanking the vaulted ceilings of the church, and the bowl of its fifteenth-century font is also borne aloft by angels.

Besides the tomb of Sir John and Florence Wyndham, another notable memorial – to Henry Wyndham (1583-1613) and his brother George (1592-1624) – may be seen set into the chancel wall. The siblings are represented in effigy, knelt in prayer. There is also a memorial brass to Edmund Wyndham (originally spelt Windham) who died on 12th November

1616. He is shown as standing at prayer, attired in full plate armour but without a helmet.

Brass of Lady Florence Wyndham, St Decuman's, Watchet

St Decuman's Well, Watchet

Between the port of Watchet and the village of Williton is a field that goes by the name of Battlegore, and it is here, according to legend, that the locals did battle with invading Norsemen. The invaders were sent packing.

Watchet's parish church is named after St Decuman, and a sculpture of the saint may be seen set into its tower. As tends to be the way with such figures, not much solid is known about him, although he is thought to have been born in the seventh century, and to have died in 706. He hailed from a noble family in Pembrokeshire, and having elected to lead the solitary life of a holy hermit determined that he would cross the waters of the estuary of the Sabrina, today known as the Bristol Channel. According to legend this voyage was accomplished employing the most unorthodox of vessels, one version of the story claiming that it was a wooden hurdle, and another that it was made from his cloak. With him he took a cow, and having made landfall on the opposite coast at Watchet, resolved to fashion himself a cell. This he built on the hill that overlooks the village, the devoted cow providing him with sustenance, whilst he ministered to the sick, and preached to the locals.

One of the latter, a heathen possessed of a pronounced enmity toward the holy hermit, decided to take Decuman's life, and thus one day cut off his head. For some few moments at least, his killer must have felt a grim sense of satisfaction, but something altogether unexpected was about to happen: Decuman's corpse rose, and picked up the severed head in its hands. Off it tottered to the holy well that still may be seen down the lane from the church, and there tenderly bathed it to cleanse it of its gore and impurities. With the task accomplished, the hands restored the saint's head to its rightful place atop his neck. Thus was the body made whole again and ready for burial. His followers buried the corpse with all due ceremony on the hilltop where a church was later raised, and there it still stands to this day, albeit in a later incarnation.

St Decuman's Well, Watchet

The Gurt Worm of Shervage Wood

For almost five hundred years, the two chaps shown in the following picture, naked but for their beards, have done battle with this two-headed wyvern, which is the only one of its type that I've seen. Some aver that it represents Shervage Wood's 'Gurt Worm', but which came first, the tale of this slithering beast, or the carving, is unclear. I suspect that it was the latter. Whatever its origins it makes for a great yarn, and it runs as follows.

Of where the Gurt Worm came from, and when it came, no mention is made, but we are told that it made its home in Shervage Wood. And there, once comfortably ensconced, it began to dine. Its appetite was first announced by the disappearance of a good many ponies and sheep, as well as game, and then, having exhausted their supply, it sought a different delicacy, and took to sampling first a shepherd, and then a brace of gipsies it caught out picking berries. Did it roast them or grill them with its fiery breath? There is no mention, but it was a very hungry beast. After all, how could it have been otherwise, given that its girth was as great as that of three stout oaks? It was all very vexing for the locals.

In Crowcombe there lived an old woman who scraped a living from gathering bilberries (known in the local dialect as 'worts'), and baking from them delicious tarts and pies, but the voracious monster had put a stop to all that. It hid itself under cover of the trees, and no one would pick her fruit for fear of falling prey to the fiend, and she wasn't such a fool as to place herself in danger. But times were hard, and she was beset with worry, what with the rent being due. And then, to her good fortune, a stranger from Stogumber came: a woodman. Seeing that he too was down on his luck, she suggested that he might look into Shervage Wood and see if there was anything there that he might cut. Oh, and whilst he was at it, would he be so good as to look out for any worts? Of course! And thus he set off generously provisioned, so he thought, with cider and a little bread and cheese.

It being a warm day and the walk uphill, it was hot going, so he paused when he got to the woods and there sat down to take a swig from his firkin. And whilst he sat there, he thought he might also take a bite, and thus turned his attention to his humble repast. He was not the only one with food on his mind however. The log beneath him shifted; it moved. 'Hold a bit!' cried he, leaping to his feet and seizing his axe. And cursing the creature for moving, he brought down his blade with such force that he sliced it in two at a stroke. A profusion of blood gushed forth. One end slithered off to Kingston St Mary, and the other in the opposite direction towards Bilbrook. Unable to tie itself back together, the Gurt Worm died.

Later that day, the woodman returned. His hat filled to the brim with worts, and he told the old woman what he'd done. He made it plain that the worm's presence came as something of a surprise, so the artful old woman made a great show of pretending she'd not told him because she'd assumed that someone else must have mentioned it to him. Indeed he had, came his reply, but he'd taken no notice of the woman as everyone knew that Crowcombe folk were notorious liars.

C16th Bench End, Church of the Holy Ghost, Crowcombe

Stogursey Castle

It is unlikely that you have ever visited the Somerset village of Stogursey. No major thoroughfare passes through it, and unless you make the specific effort to visit, it is unlikely that you will ever happen upon it. Sitting upon a minor eminence, some two miles or so as the crow flies from Hinkley Point and the towering cranes that preside over the building of its new reactor, it may be thought of as the quiet 'capital' of that oft-overlooked tract of land that sits to the northwest of Bridgwater between the A39 and the sea. But if you should ever find yourself in this part of the world, and have already taken in the many delights of the neighbouring Quantock Hills, then I'd recommend that you visit. Why? For two reasons: the remains of its picturesque castle, and its impressive Norman Church. The latter even managed to lure no lesser a personage than the exiled Emperor Haile Selassie, who cut a dapper and dignified figure when he opened the village fete in 1938.

Founded during either the late eleventh or early twelfth century, the castle was never a particularly grand affair, and is thought to have originally been built in wood. The ditch surrounding this initial structure was later deepened to form a moat fed by a nearby brook, with the spoil being employed to heighten the motte. A stone keep was then raised, with the curtain walls also being rebuilt in stone during the reign of Henry II. It hosted a visit by King John in 1210, who lost whilst gambling with his host. Besieged a few years later when Falkes de Bréauté rebelled against Henry III, an order was issued for it to be destroyed in 1228. No such thing happened. The castle was extended and rebuilt in stone by the end of the century. One of its owners, by the name of Hugh de Neville of Essex, also rebelled, and had the castle taken from him. It subsequently changed hands a number of times over the ensuing centuries. Although it was reputedly burned down by Yorkists in either 1457 or 1459, the castle would linger on as a place of habitation until it became redundant as a fortified residence during the reign of Henry VIII. Ruin and picturesque desolation would be its fate.

An engraving of the castle made in 1733 shows that it had by then become tumbledown and overgrown with vegetation, a photograph from the nineteenth century showing still less of its masonry remaining. The stone had presumably been robbed out for construction purposes elsewhere in the parish. Its gatehouse, however, was restored in the early 1980s, and for those of you with deep pockets it is available as a holiday let from the Landmark Trust. For those on a more modest budget, it is possible to at least walk the short distance from the village on the public footpath, and admire both the gatehouse and the ruins from the other side of the moat.

Gatehouse and Bridge: Stogursey Castle

Stogursey Castle

St Andrew's Church, Stogursey

For a village of its modest size, Stogursey's parish church, dedicated to St Andrew, is an impressive affair with a lengthy history and much to see. Possibly built in the 1090s, but definitely before 1106, its carved capitals are stylistically similar to those found in eleventh-century Normandy, with their decoration akin to that found at Durham (c. 1072) and Canterbury Cathedrals (c. 1075). Furthermore, the herringbone technique used in the masonry of the tower is typical of the Anglo-Saxon period, and seldom encountered after 1100. However, as with all churches its appearance would undergo many changes over the centuries, and its spire was likely added in the thirteenth century.

A priory was established here by 1120 by monks from Lonlay in Normandy, and was originally named Stoke Courcy Priory. Over the years the local accent worked its magic and Stoke Courcy gradually gave way to Stogursey.

In 1326 the then Bishop of Bath and Wells, Drokensford, paid a visit to the priory and was far from impressed. He found only a single monk in residence, as well as the Prior, and a number of 'servants and useless folk'. The other monks, to his disgust, had decamped elsewhere where they were found to be 'living lecherously'. Thus was he moved to write to the Abbot of Lonlay, who shortly thereafter took delivery of those who had strayed for the purpose of their correction.

In 1414, with England still embroiled in the Hundred Years' War, the Crown sequestrated all alien priories which were dissolved by an act of parliament. And so it was that in 1440 it was gifted to Eton College upon the latter's foundation by Henry VI, being one of a number priories so disposed of to provide a regular stream of revenue for the school. Whereas at this time it may have been deemed desirable to rupture longstanding ties with the priory's Norman parent house, national feeling had not yet risen so far for it to be deemed acceptable for one John Verney of Fairfield, a local squire, to interrupt the high mass to preach to the congregation 'in English'. In July 1442 he was summoned to appear before the Archbishop of Canterbury to account for his outrageous behaviour.

There were long rumours locally that a secret passage existed, running from the church to the now vanished priory. Indeed, an excavation of a tunnel at nearby Priory Farm took place in 1941. It was found to be three feet wide and to possess walls of an equal thickness, but a section was less than three feet high, prompting the conclusion that it was merely a mediaeval drain. However, such a substantial drain, it has been pointed out, seems outsized for a monastic community of only a dozen souls, and it has also been noted that it points in the direction of a door in the church's south transept. Whatever it was, it has now been infilled and sealed off for the sack of safety.

Further excavations in the church itself commenced in 1939. These revealed another 'mystery', in the form of a considerable number of skulls taken from beneath the floor of the crossing, some of which 'had charred flesh adhering to them'. No complete skeletons were found. For some reason, the Revd. Tucker, who had initiated and overseen the excavation, proposed the somewhat fanciful notion that these remains were clear evidence of 'human sacrifice'. Quite why he came to be possessed of this conviction, rather than opting for a rather more prosaic interpretation of viewing the deceased as having been the victims of some catastrophic fire, I do not know. A complete skeleton, however, did come to light beneath the floor between the font and the apse, this time ensconced within a grave carved into the bedrock. Water from a spring ran through it, and the foundations of a now lost square structure that stood on the site before the foundation of the church he interpreted as evidence of an erstwhile 'pagan temple'.

Although visually unassuming, there is a rusted iron ring set into one of the piers of the crossing. Popular tradition has it that this is a sanctuary ring, although such rings were normally attached to church doors. The right of sanctuary was one which survived until it was finally abolished by an act of parliament in 1623, and it is reputed that it was put to use once in this very church, when in 1243 John de Rechich availed himself of this right. John had been charged with murder, but before his trial could commence he absented himself and made for Stoke Courcy (the then name for Stogursey). As to what then became of him, local tradition makes no mention.

Nothing else quite so dramatic appears to have taken place here in St Andrew's, although it seems that the patience of a number of parishioners was tested to breaking point on more than one occasion during the reign of the first Elizabeth. A curate from nearby Lilstock was sometimes apt to preach in the church, and once droned on for so long that a certain Thomas Welley yelled out: 'Tis tyme to come down and tis tyme for our maydes to goe a milkynge.' Likewise, an Elizabeth Salye was unable to hold her tongue when he insisted on remaining in the pulpit for a full three hours one Sunday afternoon. Another parishioner – John Whelleck – was excommunicated in 1623 for causing a disturbance in the church.

Stogursey boasts a particularly fine collection of carved bench ends, and for once we are in possession of the identity of the carver: a certain fellow by the name of Glosse, whom it is believed created most, if not all, of these 33 surviving pieces between the years 1524 and 1529. Amongst the most eye-catching of these are the following: a depiction of a man, naked but for a loincloth grasping two strands of foliage; a spoonbill; a sinuous dragon-like creature from which sprout a number of leaves; seahorses with human heads; and the pelican feeding its young from the blood of its breast, although it cannot be said to resemble a pelican. Other curiosities include two fonts, one of which dates from the Norman period; the fossil of an ichthyosaurus which was moved to the church in 1944; an impressive bier which has been displayed her since 1919; and the mediaeval tombs of two members of the Verney family. Both of the latter are surmounted by effigies, the older and cruder carving dating from 1333 and showing William de Verney holding his heart, and the more recent, carved after the death of John de Verney in 1447, being an accomplished and detailed piece showing the deceased lord laid out in prayerful aspect clad in plate armour.

All in all, St Andrew's is a church which holds much history and interest. If you should have time having visited the church and the castle, then you may wish to try and track down a local Bronze Age barrow, for an unusual piece of folklore is attached to it. Its name is Wick Barrow, and since time immemorial it has possessed an association with the pixies. There is, however, only one anecdote attached to it that I know of, although when the alleged events are said to have taken place is unclear. The story goes that one day a ploughman overheard what he took to be a young child crying and complaining amidst the bushes that topped the barrow. The cause of the upset, it transpired, was that the child had broken its 'peel'. Curious, the ploughman made his way through the undergrowth only to find that the discarded peel (a shovel used for baking bread) was of an exceptionally small size. Its handle had been broken, but there was no sign of the child. Thinking it nothing more than a toy, he fixed it, and left it at the spot where he had found it. When his labours were over at the day's end he returned to see if the toy had been reclaimed. Indeed it had, and in its place he found a delicious hot cake, freshly baked from the pixies' oven.

Tucked away at the end of a short alley leading off of Stogursey's high street may be found St Andrew's Well. For quite how long it has been regarded as holy no one knows, but it was first mentioned by name in 1473. Even though the village is sat on a low hill of no great height, and the well near its top, an abundant and strong flow of clear water pours forth from the two springs by which it is fed. It is said that the springs have never been known to fail. It is thought that the archway over its gate dates from the second half of the eighteenth century, built by the Egment family who purchased the manor of Stogursey in 1757.

Although neither magical nor healing qualities are claimed on their behalf, the waters of the well are said to have been particularly good for drinking. Despite their origins in sources so close to each other, they run through two separate cisterns, with the water issuing from the right-hand spring believed to be softer and therefore more suited to the washing of clothes. Nearby, back on the high street, may be seen a stone stump, which is all that remains of a mediaeval cross.

St Andrew's Well, Stogursey

Tomb of John de Verney (died 1447), St Andrew's, Stogursey

Carved Capital, St Andrew's, Stogursey

Carved Capital, St Andrew's, Stogursey

Funeral Bier, St Andrew's, Stogursey

Sixteenth-century Bench End, St Andrew's, Stogursey

Sixteenth-century Bench End, St Andrew's, Stogursey

Wedmore's Haunted History

Wedmore is a characterful and historic village, and has in recent years become something of a sought-after location with eye-watering property prices to match. It sits on the edge of a raised area of land named the Isle of Wedmore, which before the drainage of the surrounding Somerset Levels was often difficult to access owing to the swampy and waterlogged nature of the terrain. Its parish church, dedicated to St Mary with sections dating back to the twelfth century, is its oldest visible structure. There was, however, an earlier church on this site, and it was here in 878 that what became known as the Treaty of Wedmore was solemnised between King Alfred of Wessex and the defeated Danish leader, Guthrum. The latter had been baptised some eight days earlier at nearby Aller, and it was at Wedmore that his baptismal rite was finalised with the unbinding of the chrisom. Twelve days of feasting ensued.

No other aspect of the village's history would have such significance for the country that would one day become England, but like many Somerset parishes, it would be touched adversely by the fallout from the abortive Sedgemoor Rebellion of 1685. There is a local tradition that the notorious Judge Jeffreys held court here at the George Inn, and as is often the case with the Hanging Judge, his restless shade is said to still haunt it. The pub also claims to be frequented by the spirit of an Edwardian lady dressed in grey, whilst the ghost of Dr John Westover, a pioneer in the humane treatment of mental illness who died in 1706, is also said to appear in the doorway of his old home, West End.

Church of St Mary, Wedmore

South Yorkshire
The Shrewsbury Chapel of Sheffield Cathedral
Two of the monumental tombs in Sheffield Cathedral are of particular note, both dating from the sixteenth century when it was still a 'humble' parish church. The earlier of the two belongs to George Talbot, 4th Earl of Shrewsbury (1468-1538), and his two wives Anne and Elizabeth. It was he who added the Shrewsbury Chapel to the church in 1520, which is when it is thought his first wife Anne died. He fought on the side of King Henry VII at the Battle of Stoke in 1487, and two years later ventured to Flanders as part of an English expeditionary force which fought on the side of the Holy Roman Emperor against the French. His star shone brightly at the Tudor court, and in 1512 he was Lieutenant-General of the English army in France, taking part in the Battle of the Spurs the following year. He supported Henry VIII's divorce of Katherine of Aragon and his moves against Cardinal Wolsey, but provided hospitality for the cardinal as he travelled south from York having been arrested for treason. Talbot remained loyal during the Pilgrimage of Grace, his forces playing a significant role in saving Henry's throne.

His tomb is opulent. The chest itself looks rather the worse for wear, but the alabaster effigies have survived well. As with the majority of high-status tombs of this era, it would originally have been brightly pigmented.

The second grand monument commemorates George Talbot, 6th Earl of Shrewsbury (1528-1590), the fourth and final husband of Bess of Hardwick. However, whereas he lies here in the Shrewsbury Chapel, his wife, who survived him by eighteen years, lies in Derby. This distant physical separation is telling.

Talbot acceded to the Earldom of Shrewsbury in 1560, the year he became Chamberlain of the Exchequer, a position previously held by his father. The following year he became a Knight of the Garter. His first wife, Lady Gertrude Manners, died in January 1567, but he wasted no time in remarrying Bess of Hardwick, for the two were wed in the February of the following year. Although she possessed great wealth, as did he, he soon came to rue the personal aspect of this union, if not its financial one.

From 1568, Queen Elizabeth I placed Mary Queen of Scots under his custody, a responsibility that made considerable financial demands upon the Earl, and, it is said, contributed to the ruination of his health over the fifteen years for which he was responsible for the exiled Queen. The allowance provided by the Crown for Mary's care at Sheffield Castle, although inadequate, was cut from £52 to £30 per week after Shrewsbury made it known that he was being ruined by the expense of keeping the exiled monarch. Mary spent with carefree abandon, and seemed to revel in wanton waste and disrespect for his property. It is no wonder that he grew increasingly irascible, with his health doing little to alleviate the state of his temper, for he was plagued by chronic rheumatism. And if this were not bad enough, his relations with his wife became ever more embittered.

Relations between the Earl and Bess had already turned decidedly sour by 1574, when she, together with the Countess Lennox, arranged a wedding between Elizabeth Cavendish and Charles Stuart, Earl of Lennox, without her husband's knowledge. This match placed Bess's daughter, and any of her subsequent children, in line of succession to the throne. Shrewsbury, ignorant of his wife's machinations until the deed had been done, wrote grovelling letters to Lord Burghley and to the Queen, seeking to exonerate his name from any involvement in the affair, for he knew that this was sure to meet with royal censure. Indeed, the marriage did meet with royal displeasure, but luckily for him he avoided imprisonment by a hair's breadth, as well as the confiscation of his estates. Worse, however, was to come.

A rumour later arose that Shrewsbury had enjoyed an 'improper relationship' with Mary Stuart, and even that she had had a child by him. When he learnt of the existence of this dangerous and harmful gossip, he wrote to Elizabeth, accusing his wife of having fabricated these allegations. Upon investigation, it was revealed that his wife had indeed been the source of these false rumours. He was charged with, but cleared of, treason in 1584. It would be no exaggeration to say that by this point he had come to loathe his spouse. However, Elizabeth ordered him to visit his wife, despite his objections. This did nothing to repair their relations, and the estrangement between the pair festered until his death. During these last years of his life, he sought and found emotional solace in his mistress Eleanor Britton, who was with him when he died on 18 November 1590. Her station was not nearly as elevated as that of Bess, for she had been a servant at Hardwick Hall.

Tomb of George Talbot, 6th Earl of Shrewsbury

Tomb of George Talbot, 6th Earl of Shrewsbury

Tomb of George Talbot, 4th Earl of Shrewsbury

Thornseat Lodge

If any house I've set eyes upon resembles the archetypal haunted house, it's this one: Thornseat (also formerly known as Thornsett) Lodge in South Yorkshire. It speaks of the wealth of the high Victorian era, having been built by the Jessops, a family of steel-making magnates from nearby Sheffield, who acquired the 109-acre estate upon which Thornsett was to be built in 1852. It is thought that the lodge was built by Sidney Jessop in about 1855 as a grouse-shooting retreat, but no record survives of either the identity of its architect, or the precise date of its construction.

It remained in the ownership of the Jessop family until it was sold off in 1933, and in 1939 became a children's home, which it remained, in one form or another, until its closure in 1980. It was in 1939 that the Lodge's name was changed from Thornsett to Thornseat. Thereafter, Thornseat began its slide into dereliction, although as recently as the early 1990s it was open for low-income Sheffield families to enjoy holidays there. Any plans for its future remain uncertain, but as can be seen from this picture, elements of its primary fabric are now becoming unstable, and subject to collapse.

Something in the Cellar of the Three Tuns Inn

Sheffield boasts a remarkable number of fine real ale pubs, amongst which numbers the Three Tuns Inn. A hostelry has stood on this site since at least the 1700s, and has, for one reason or another, experienced an unusually rapid turnover of landlords in recent years. This is probably, I should imagine, expressive of the difficulties of running a city-centre pub in today's challenging economic environment, even before the impact of the recent lockdowns and raging inflation in energy costs have been factored into the equation. Others, however, have suggested an alternative reason for its succession of short tenures: the supernatural.

In this instance, it is not the public bar that is said to provide the location for the alleged haunting, but rather its cellar. Dogs and cats reputedly shun the wooden steps that lead into its depths, and a number of people who have ventured down to change the barrels have reported a variety of strange experiences. During the early hours of the morning, a number of people have reported that the sound of a sobbing woman might be heard there. She seems somewhat coy, however, for she does not allow herself to be seen. But the presence does announce itself in other ways than sobbing alone. A visiting contractor, feeling the gentle touch of a hand upon his shoulder, looked round to find no one there. So discomfited was he by this experience that he promptly downed tools and refused to return. For others, a visit to the cellar has precipitated a sudden attack of shivering, or sweating, and a desire to flee its confined space as soon as possible.

Whatever the atmosphere of the cellar may be like, that of the bar itself is decidedly agreeable, with nothing stranger to be seen than a pint of 'Old Peculier'.

The Three Tuns Inn, Sheffield

Staffordshire
The Church of the Holy Cross, Ilam
The Legend of St Bertram

In the Church of the Holy Cross in Ilam may be seen a tomb reputed to belong to the Mercian Saint Bertram, who by tradition is said to have died in the eighth century. As to who Bertram was, and what he did, no written source of his life and deeds was compiled until a number of centuries after his death, so their facts may be somewhat questionable, as is so often the case with such shadowy figures from this period. Indeed, Bertram's shrine itself dates from the fourteenth century, although owing to the amount of clutter placed upon its surface it bears something of a resemblance to an untidy occasional table.

It is said that Bertram was born into the Mercian royal family, and whilst a young man travelled to Ireland where he fell in love with, and married, a princess whom he brought back to his home country. He subsequently had a son by her, and they took shelter in Thor's Cave in Wetton. Whilst out one day gathering food for his young family, wolves found their way into their rocky home and killed both his wife and child. Devastated by his loss, he adopted the ascetic life of a holy man and devoted himself to God, preaching to the pagan inhabitants of Staffordshire. He eventually took up residence in another cave in Ilam, and there he lived until he died. Tradition states that the Devil sought to tempt him by turning stones into bread, but the saint did not succumb to his display of power.

The shrine that you see on the next page houses the saint's relics, and is said to have worked many a miraculous cure. It continues to be a site of pilgrimage to this day, with Bertram also attracting pilgrims from the Orthodox Church.

St Bertram's Tomb, Church of the Holy Cross, Ilam

Two Monuments, One Family

Also to be found in the church are two fine monuments dedicated to the memory of two generations of the same family. The finest of the pair is a chest tomb, surmounted by alabaster effigies of Robert and Elizabeth Meverell, whilst above on the wall is a monument to their daughter and her three children. Man and wife both died in 1626, with Robert dying on 5th February, followed by Elizabeth on 5th August. It would seem that Elizabeth came from the more illustrious family, for her father, Sir Thomas Fleming, was Lord Chief Justice of the King's Bench at the time of the couple's marriage. It was Fleming who presided as judge at the trial of Guy Fawkes. Their daughter, who was the last of the Meverells, went on to marry the 1st Earl of Ardglass, the great-great grandson of Hilary Mantel's 'favourite', Thomas Cromwell. The stately home of the Meverells – Throwley Old Hall, situated near the Staffordshire village of Calton – now lies in ruins. Strangely, although there is a monument dedicated to the younger Elizabeth Meverell and her four children against the wall above her parents, she was actually buried along with her husband, Thomas Cromwell, in Blore, Staffordshire.

Tomb of Robert and Elizabeth Meverell

Effigies of Elizabeth Cromwell's Four Young Children

Monument to Elizabeth Cromwell, née Meverell

The church also possesses a fascinating Anglo-Norman font. Dating from the twelfth century, its iconography is crudely executed, but the carving of a beast has been identified as the dragon named Behemoth, whose raised coiled tail is intended to signify the end of the world.

In the churchyard are the heavily weathered shafts of two Anglo-Saxon crosses. Little of their original decorative detail is now discernible, and they are believed to date to the tenth century. As for the church itself, it has been heavily restored and remodelled over the course of its history, with the bulk of its current visible structure dating from the 19th and 17th centuries, although its origins lie in the period before the Norman Conquest.

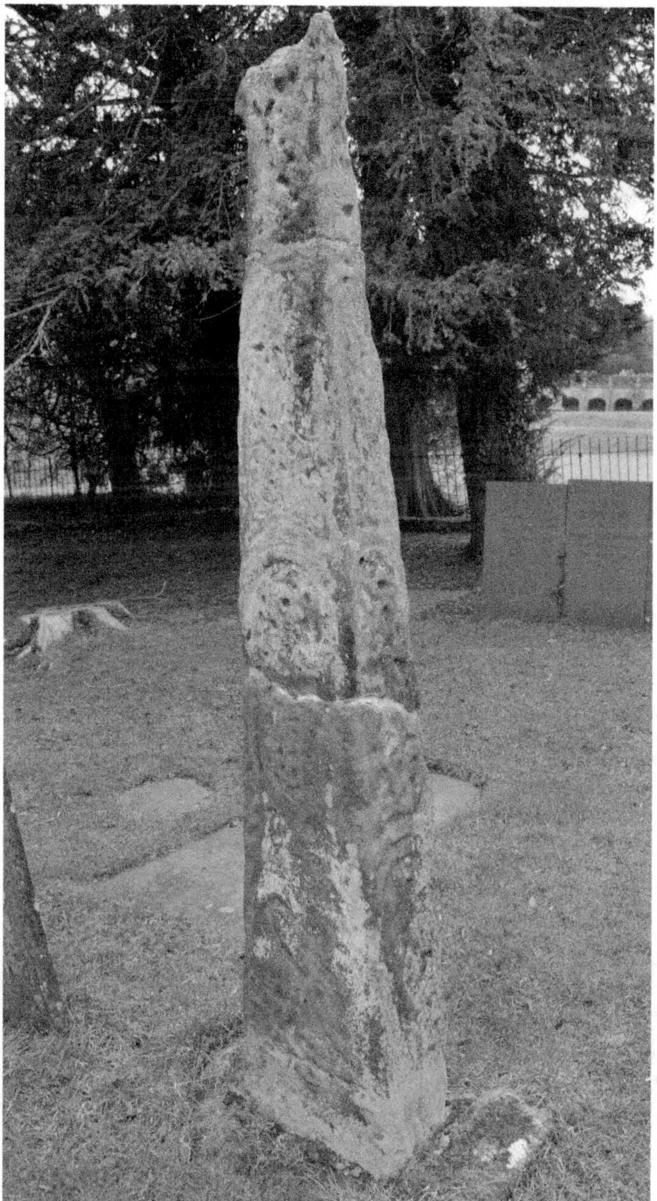

Font, Holy Cross Church, Ilam

Leek's Pre-Conquest Crosses

Although the oldest part of the extant fabric of St Edward's Church in the town of Leek in Staffordshire dates back no further than the thirteenth century, its churchyard hosts two crosses from the early-mediaeval period. Unfortunately, as the church was locked on the day of my visit, I was unable to venture inside and view the other pieces of carved stonework from the pre-Conquest period, so all I have are these pictures of the two crosses that stand outside.

Neither of the crosses can be dated with any certainty, but they are both believed to date from the seventh to eleventh centuries. As the first of them shown on the next page is characterised as Anglo-Norse in design, this would suggest a date no earlier than the latter part of the ninth century when the area was subject to Danish overlordship. Sadly, much of the original decoration has eroded away, and its original base which possessed a Latin inscription has now been replaced with a modern one made of concrete.

The second cross has, to a certain extent, fared even less favourably in terms of its preservation over the centuries, and has been reassembled from three large sections; much of its original fabric is missing. There is said to be a runic inscription at its base, but this is so badly worn that I did not notice its presence when I took the pictures.

There is a local saying: 'When the churchyard cross shall disappear, Leek town will not last another year.' Although both crosses may be seen to be well past their prime, it would seem that Leek will survive for some while yet.

Anglo-Norse Cross, St Edward's Churchyard, Leek

Anglo-Norse Cross, St Edward's Churchyard, Leek

Haunted Leek

Leek is reputed to be haunted by a spook or two, its older hostelries being the preferred location for some of them. Given that the Roebuck Hotel has stood in the town since 1626, it should perhaps come as no surprise to learn that, as with many inns of such an age, it possesses a reputation for being haunted. In this instance it would seem that a former landlord remains so attached to the place that he cannot bear to leave it, although neither his identity, nor the date of his death, are recorded. As for the Roebuck's stairs, it is reported that they are the favoured haunt of an affable spirit named Harry, although quite how he came to acquire his friendly reputation is likewise unrecorded.

Another of Leek's pubs dating from the seventeenth century – the Green Dragon – was once used as a regular watering hole by J.R.R. Tolkien when visiting the neighbouring Staffordshire moorlands. His quiet spirit is alleged to have been spotted in the pub at least once since his death.

There is, however, one ghost story associated with the town which does not involve a pub, and possesses a colourful if somewhat gruesome genesis. The restless spirit in question is said to be that of John Nadin, or Naden, an agricultural labourer who murdered his master, a farmer by the name of Robert Brough, in August 1731. It would appear that there was no initial enmity between the two men, quite the contrary in fact, for the two were said to have got on amicably enough, with Nadin even saving the farmer from drowning when he fell into the River Dane. Their problems arouse as a consequence of Robert's wife Julia getting on even better with Nadin than her husband, for it is said that she fell in love with him, and having whispered so many sweet nothings into Nadin's ear led him to murder his employer. The deed done, she then betrayed him to the law and he was sentenced to death for murder after a short trial in Stafford. He choked his last swinging from a gallows erected within sight of Brough's door. His body was then cut down, daubed with pitch, and exhibited in a gibbet that hung upon Gun Hill. There it was left until it eventually rotted away, and the disarticulated bones fell apart. The gibbet itself was still standing on the hill in the 1870s, although no trace of it now remains.

What became of Nadin's bones? Were they gathered up and spirited away? Was his hand taken and used by housebreakers in their nefarious business as a hand of glory? Whatever happened to his bones, a number of rumours grew up regarding his spirit. One story has it that after the gallows were dismantled the wood was put to good use in fashioning a number of stiles in the countryside thereabouts, and Naden's ghost has since been witnessed stepping over them, wandering between Danebridge, Wincle and Bosley in nearby Cheshire. A ghostly black dog – a padfoot – is also held to haunt Gun Hill. Folklore explains that these hellish hounds stand sentinel over some place of violent death, or over a place of burial. Indeed, three locations not so far from Leek up on the moorlands are said to be frequented by padfoots. These stand guard over the graves of slain Jacobites, who made it no further in their long retreat back to Scotland from Derby. But in the case of this particular shaggy dog story, no hound has been reported as either standing guard over, or feasting and gnawing upon Nadin's bones.

The Roebuck Hotel, Leek

Almshouses, Leek

Suffolk

The Riotous Past of Bury St Edmunds Abbey Gatehouses

Ruinous. That would be a fair description of the state of Bury St Edmunds Abbey today. Founded in 1020 at a shrine to the martyred King of East Anglia from whom it took its name, its wealth and prestige would grow until it met its end in 1539 when it fell victim to the Henrician Dissolution. Little now remains as testimony to its splendour, although two of its gatehouses - the Norman Tower and the Abbey Gate - provide a hint of its former glory. And these two structures, architecturally impressive as they are, also serve as a repository of mute memory for the events that played out about them during the town's turbulent history.

As its name would suggest, it is the former that is the older of the pair, having been built between 1120 and 1148, with the Abbey Gate a mere youngster by comparison. Perhaps the latter's original form was not so different to that of the Norman Tower, but it was rebuilt in the mid-fourteenth century following the 'Great Riot' of 1327, having failed in its function of protecting the abbey precinct. The violence associated with this event was an expression of pent-up popular resentment, the townsfolk having wearied of the perceived privileges enjoyed, and exploited, by the abbot and his monks. It began in January, and would continue well into the autumn, resulting in loss of life, and destruction of property. This assault upon the abbey's inhabitants and fabric provided a foretaste of what was to be visited upon it two centuries later, albeit at the behest of the state, rather than of the local populace.

The January violence succeeded in compelling the abbey to grant a charter of liberties to the town's secular inhabitants, but as it was extracted under duress, it was withdrawn at the earliest possible opportunity the following month. Popular ire once more exploded, fuelling more attacks in February and May. Records were seized and destroyed, those detailing debtors' accounts presumably being consigned to oblivion with the greatest savour. Queen Isabella, at the head of an army come to England to depose Edward II, stopped here at the end of September, and so hostilities ceased. For a while.

In October, a party of monks stripped off their habits to reveal the armour that they wore below, and took hostages in Bury's parish church. In the ensuing violence they killed a number of parishioners, prompting the townsfolk to at last rise up and storm the abbey. It was during this final frenzied attack that the gates were burned, and the abbey fell into secular hands. Thus would the Abbey Gate later be rebuilt with defensive considerations uppermost in mind, and its portcullis remains for all to see to this day.

As for the Norman Tower, it is still in use, for it serves as the belfry of the neighbouring Church of St James, now reborn as St Edmundsbury Cathedral. However, its survival at once looked in doubt, but not because of the hostile actions of the local populace. It long served as a bell tower, and by the beginning of the nineteenth century the ringing of the bells appears to have contributed to its instability. Part of its eastern face collapsed after the bells were rung on 5 November 1818, but the cracks were plastered over and the ringing continued. Additional pieces of masonry fell away in 1843, and substantial works were thus initiated in 1844 to finally stabilise the structure. They were completed at the close of 1848, and the tower has remained solid ever since.

The pictures on the following page show the fourteenth-century gatehouse, and those one the following two the Norman Tower.

237

238

The Curiosities of Hadleigh

Although far from the centre of events today, the Suffolk market town of Hadleigh has borne witness to a notable occurrence or two during its lengthy history. It is thought that the churchyard of St Mary's is the resting place of the Danish King Guthrum, who took the baptismal name of Athelstan after being persuaded to convert to Christianity by King Alfred in 878. It has also been speculated that Guthrum was the church's founder, although no solid evidence exists.

Inside St Mary's may be seen a curious pair of carvings. They decorate the two ends of a wooden bench. One of them seemingly represents a lion, and the other what is thought to be an allusion to the legend of St Edmund and the discovery of his head, guarded over by a wolf. The creature that holds the bearded head between its teeth is, however, unlike any other wolf that you will have seen. Upon its head is a sort of cap or hood, and around its neck may be seen a decorative collar. Its face looks distinctly human, albeit grotesque and distorted, and upon its forelegs it wears a pair of pointed shoes. Its hindmost legs are cloven-hoofed, whereas folded onto its back would appear to be a pair of wings most closely resembling those of a bat. It is a unique chimerical fancy.

The most famous rector of St Mary's – Dr Rowland Taylor – was to meet a terrible end. He had the misfortune to live at a time when the concept of religious tolerance was anathema to the Crown. Appointed to his position in the parish of Hadleigh by Archbishop Thomas Cranmer in 1544, he was a fervent Protestant and supporter of the newly-formed Church of England. The accession of Queen Mary in 1553, therefore, cannot have been greeted with any sense of enthusiasm. Indeed, so hot was he in defence of his beliefs that he had something of an altercation inside St Mary's with the Catholic priest of neighbouring Aldham. Affronted, the latter would come to have his revenge.

Dr Taylor was tried in London by Bishop Stephen Gardiner and condemned to death on 30th January 1555. On 9th February he was led to Aldham Common where he was tied to a stake and burned for heresy, the first to suffer such a fate under the new queen. His curate, Richard Yeomans, would also burn for heresy in 1558. For the time being at least, such violence is thankfully behind us, although the concept of punishing 'heretics' of one sort or another has sadly undergone something of a recent revival.

Although Dr Rowland's violent end does not appear to have spawned any ghostly folklore, the road between Hadleigh and Layham has the reputation of being haunted by a woman named Mary, a suicide. Her grave lies somewhere along its length, presumably at a crossroads. I know of no further details. One other haunting is noted. The landlord of the White Lion in Hadleigh reported waking one evening in 1979 to find an old man in his bedroom. There is no record of what this stranger did or said, if indeed anything, but the witness was convinced that it was a ghost, which was probably less alarming than finding a living and breathing old man in his room. It happened only the once, with the landlord having formed the impression that the old chap was a seaman. Sleep paralysis?

Bench End, St Mary's Church, Hadleigh

St Mary's Church, Hadleigh

The Lost Treasure of Ickworth House

Just south of Bury St Edmunds stands the imposing edifice of Ickworth House, its most notable feature being its enormous rotunda from which radiate two great wings. Built between 1795 and 1829, Frederick Hervey, the 4th Earl of Bristol, had intended that it should primarily function as a gallery for his extensive art collection, but his plans were thwarted by Napoleon's seizing of his treasures. Even so, Ickworth today provides a home to many paintings of note. However, the lost treasure alluded to in the title of this entry relates not to the world of art, but to monastic gold.

The story has come down to us thanks to an anecdote related by Lord Arthur Charles Hervey (1808-1894) in one of his papers delivered to the Bury and West Suffolk Archaeological Institute, which he at the time headed. Whether the pool that features in the story – referred to by the locals as the Golden Pond – still exists, I do not know, but this is where one of the abbots of Bury St Edmunds is said to have deposited his gold in an effort to prevent it being stolen. This tale was allegedly substantiated when a chest containing what was thought to be the lost treasure was dredged up from the bottom of the pond. One can hardly imagine the sense of excitement exhibited by its finders, nor their sense of abject disappointment as the chest slid back into the waters after they had hauled it up onto the bank. What happened then? Did they manage once more to retrieve it?

There was a chest – an empty one, naturally – that was displayed at Ickworth during Lord Arthur's time, which was claimed to be the self-same one that had been found in the pond. As to what happened to its contents, well, the grandiose neoclassical structure in which it was shown must have cost a pretty penny or two. No one knows.

Given that the elusive treasure of the Golden Pond was said to have possessed ecclesiastical origins, it thus seems rather fitting that Lord Arthur himself was ordained, becoming Bishop of Bath and Wells in 1869. It is one of his daughters whom we have to thank for instituting a charming custom that continues to this day: the ringing of a bell for food by the resident mute swans that glide about the moat of Wells's Bishop's Palace.

Ickworth House

The Haunted History of the Moyse's Hall Museum
It would be true to say that the picture which follows fails to do justice to the building that it shows – Moyse's Hall in Bury St Edmunds. It has stood here on the edge of the marketplace for some eight-and-a-half centuries or more, and in that time has fulfilled a great many purposes. Since the close of the nineteenth century it has been a museum, but long before that it served the community in a number of less appealing guises: a prison, a workhouse, and a police station.

And it is this lengthy history, and its centrality to the town's civic life, that has perhaps furnished it with something more than mere memories. It would be surprising, therefore, if it had not acquired the reputation of being haunted, and for those who enjoy the frisson of sensing a cold touch, or a chill breath from beyond the grave, then perhaps it will not disappoint.

Moyse's Hall is home to a very old ghost story indeed, for in 1328 a woman was reported as having seen 'a most horrible devil' in its cellar. Reports of more recent sightings are, however, thin on the ground to non-existent. But it is a set of supernatural occurrences linked to a notorious crime committed towards the close of the Georgian period for which it is better known. The criminal said to have spawned these disturbances was William Corder, 'the Red Barn Murderer,' hanged in 1828 for the brutal murder of his lover, Maria Martin. As a rather ghoulish postscript, not only was a death mask taken from his corpse, but his body was partly flayed and his skin tanned. This skin was then used to bind an account of his crime.

At that time, Moyse's Hall still served as a gaol, and after Corder's execution found itself beset by ghostly apparitions and terrifying shrieks that continued until the decision was taken to bury his skull. And with its burial came a sudden peace. As for the book, it remains on display in the museum along with the murderer's death mask.

For those of you with an interest in the history of witchcraft and the terrifying and bloody witch trials that took place in seventeenth-century Bury, you will find certain material within Moyse's Hall Museum of interest. The gibbet looks pretty grim too.

Moyse's Hall Museum, Bury St Edmunds

West Yorkshire
The Ghost of Benjamin Ferrand, St Ives, Bingley

Just outside of the town of Bingley on top of a hill sits the St Ives Estate. It once belonged to the wealthy Ferrand family, but was sold to Bingley Urban District Council in 1928, but the story I am about to recount took place many years earlier, and concerns the single instance of a haunting which took place on the night of 20th October 1803.

The then master of the house, Major Benjamin Ferrand, had been away at Buxton taking the waters on account of his ill health, and having felt himself somewhat recovered decided to make his way home. However, that same evening he once again fell ill and was taken to the Cat and Fiddle Inn. There, that night, he died.

Back at the estate that evening, a number of servants of a Dr Hartley, who were walking home from the nearby village of Harden, happened to catch sight of Ferrand sat atop his distinctive white pony at the gates to the estate. Up they ran to open the gates for him, and rider and mount passed through. They related the major's return to their master that same evening, who naturally thought nothing more of it until some days later the news arrived of Ferrand's death that very night high up on the Derbyshire moors.

It is a tale that admittedly elicits a certain frisson, and although recounted by local historian Harry Speight in one of his books almost a century later, it would seem that the embellishments of folkloric memory had been at play during the intervening decades. For one, the Cat and Fiddle Inn would not be built until 1813, a full decade after Ferrand's death, and secondly, according to the estate's website, there was no Benjamin Ferrand in residence at the house at the time. A Ferrand of that name was master of the house between 1674 and 1699, but during the period in question the family had let their dwelling to a succession of tenants, only returning to live there in 1803.

Did Dr Hartley's servants really witness the return of the master of St Ives that autumn evening? Perhaps. The details may be garbled, but the story remains charming; such is the nature of folklore. As for the house, it was demolished in 1859.

Wood Nymph, the St Ives Estate, Bingley

Wiltshire

West Kennet Long Barrow: Archaeology and Folklore

Given its age, there is surprisingly little by way of folklore attached to this most famous of long barrows, so I shall start with a brief archaeological overview. Situated a mile and a half to the south of Avebury, this barrow is one of the most impressive tombs to survive from the Neolithic period. Although much of its 100-metre length has been disturbed by digging, its chambers are intact and thanks to later excavation accessible to the public. Construction is believed to have commenced in circa 3650 BC, with usage in one form or another having continued for the next millennium or so until it was purposefully infilled.

The disarticulated remains of 46 individuals of various ages have been found here, all believed to have been deposited within a relatively short timeframe of around 20-30 years. This would seem to indicate that the barrow's specific use for burial was brief, with some other, presumably ritual, purpose, soon supplanting this as its primary function.

As for the folklore, it would appear to be of rather recent origin, and it concerns a ghost of which I have happened upon only a handful of mentions. In one variant, it is said that the apparition of a man appears at the barrow on Midsummer's Eve. He is accompanied by a white hound, and the two of them are seen to make a circuit of the environs of the tomb. They are interpreted as performing some sort of guardian function. The other version of this story goes that the 'shaman' and his dog appear not on Midsummer's Eve, but on the longest and shortest days, as well as at the vernal and autumn equinoxes. As to any alleged eyewitness accounts, I have as yet to stumble upon one.

West Kennet Long Barrow

Entrance to West Kennet Long Barrow

Select Bibliography

For the sake of brevity only the book/article title and author name together with date of publication have been included for each entry. A number of the older titles listed are out of copyright and freely available online.

British Folk-Tales and Legends, Katharine Briggs, 1977.
Bygone Cumberland and Westmorland, Daniel Scott, 1899.
Chronicles and Stories of Old Bingley, Harry Speight, 1898.
County Folk-Lore of Suffolk, ed. Lady Eveline Camilla Gurdon, 1895.
County Folk-Lore Vol. II North Riding of Yorkshire, York and the Ainsty, ed. Mrs Gutch, 1901.
The Fairies in Tradition and Literature, Katharine Briggs, 1967.
Folklore, Myths and Legends of Britain, Readers Digest, 1973.
Legends and Superstitions of the County of Durham, William Brockie, 1886.
Myths, Scenes, & Worthies of Somerset, Mrs E. Boger, 1887.
Notes on the Folk-Lore of the Northern Counties of England and the Borders, William Henderson, 1879.
Religion and the Decline of Magic, Keith Thomas, 1971.
St Bega – Cult, Fact and Legend, John M. Todd, 1980.
Tradition and Folklore of the Quantocks, the Rev. Chas. Whistler, 1907.

Recommended Websites
Britain Express
British History Online
The History of Parliament
Great English Churches
Historic England
The Paranormal Database

Printed in Dunstable, United Kingdom